MINDING MIND

Also by THOMAS CLEARY

The Blue Cliff Record, with J. C. Cleary (1977, 1992)*
The Flower Ornament Scripture (1984–1987, 1993)*
Shōbōgenzō: Zen Essays of Dōgen (1986)
Zen Essence: The Science of Freedom (1989)*
Zen Lessons: The Art of Leadership (1989)*
Transmission of Light, by Zen Master Keizan (1990)
No Barrier, by Mumon (1993)
Rational Zen: The Mind of Dōgen Zenji (1993)*
Zen Antics: 101 Stories of Enlightenment (1993)*
Dream Conversations: On Buddhism and Zen,
by Musō Kokushi (1994)*
Zen Letters: Teachings of Yuanwu,
with J. C. Cleary (1994)*

*Published by Shambhala Publications

MINDING MIND

A COURSE IN BASIC MEDITATION

Translated and Explained by

THOMAS CLEARY

SHAMBHALA
Boston & London
1995

Shambhala Publications, Inc.
Horticultural Hall
300 Massachusetts Avenue
Boston, Massachusetts 02115
http://www.shambhala.com

9 8 7 6 5 4 3

Printed in the United States of America
⊗ This edition is printed on acid-free paper that meets the
American National Standards Institute Z39.48 Standard.
Distributed in the United States by Random House, Inc.,
and in Canada by Random House of Canada Ltd

Library of Congress Cataloging-in-Publication Data

Minding mind: a course in basic meditation/translated and
explained by Thomas Cleary.—1st ed.
        p.   cm.   ISBN 1-57062-004-0
1. Meditation—Buddhism.   I. Cleary, Thomas F., 1949– .
        BQ5612.M56   1995   94-27845
        294.3'443—dc20   CIP

CONTENTS

TRANSLATOR'S INTRODUCTION

> Let the wise one watch over the mind,
>   so hard to perceive, so artful,
>   alighting where it wishes;
> a watchfully protected mind
>   will bring happiness.
>   —*Dhammapada*

> Sages use the mind deliberately,
>   based on its essence.
> With the support of the spirit,
>   they finish what they begin.
> Thus they sleep without dreams
>   and wake without troubles.
>   —*Huainanzi*

Conscious cultivation of consciousness has been practiced by human beings for thousands of years, giving rise to many traditional sciences of mental development whose origins are lost in the dimness of the early dawn twilight of human awareness. Buddhist tradition is based on a breakthrough made by Siddhartha Gautama twenty-five hundred years ago in his attempts to rediscover the essential way to *moksha*, liberation, and *bodhi*, enlightenment, lost ideals of ancient tradition.

The mental science of Buddhism is extremely rich and complex. It is not simply an outgrowth, reformulation, or development of ancient Indian religion. According to Buddhist lore, there are five general categories of practice by which the relations and differences among orientations and methods of meditation can be distinguished.

The first type is called the meditation of the ordinary mortal. The intention and purpose of this type of meditation is to enhance the ordinary perceptions and faculties of the individual. The desired result is greater efficacy and efficiency in the ordinary activities of life, leading to a sense of confidence and well-being.

The second type of meditation is quite different from the first, focusing on transcending the world rather than dealing with the world in conventional terms. The desired result is quiescent nirvana, a profound peace of mind characterized by extinction of psychological afflictions. Exceptional psychic capacities are also commonly associated with people who attain quiescent nirvana in this way, but because they habitually remain in the quiescence of individual nirvana they do not ordinarily exercise these capacities in a concerted manner.

The third type of meditation focuses on the cultivation of altered states of consciousness. Those who practice meditation for the sake of attaining nirvana may also use these altered states for the purpose of breaking attachments to conceptual and perceptual conventions, but they are thereby exposed to the danger of addiction to intoxicating trances. Buddhist teaching emphasizes sobriety to avoid being obsessed, or as it is said, "reborn under the sway" of unusual states, taking care to use them for specific pragmatic purposes rather than for self-indulgence.

The fourth kind of meditation is dedicated to development of extraordinary capacities in the service of other people and the world at large. Practitioners of this type of meditation may use any or all of the methods and techniques characteristic of the first three kinds of meditation, but with a different orientation, in a different manner, and in a broader context. The range and scope of meditational states and experiences in this fourth category, furthermore, exceed those of the lower types of meditation by many orders of magnitude.

The fifth and highest type of meditation, according to this ancient classification, is called pure clear meditation arriving at being-as-is. This is considered the most penetrating insight and the nearest that an individual consciousness can come to true objectivity. The realization of pure clear meditation also enables its master to employ all the other types of meditation method deliberately and freely, without becoming fixated or obsessed.

Minding Mind is a compendium of instruction manuals dealing primarily with ways of attaining to the mode of experience characteristic of the last-named type of meditation, pure clear meditation arriving at being-as-is.

The first manual, *Treatise on the Supreme Vehicle,* is attributed to Hongren (602–675), who is known as the Fifth Patriarch of Chan Buddhism in China. There appears to be no historical trace of this text previous to the sixteenth century, and its origins are obscure. Although Hongren, like his teacher and several of his own disciples, was an illustrious Chan master of his time, little is really known for sure about his teaching or the activities of his school.

The language of this meditation manual would also suggest that it was in fact written in the sixteenth century, although certain passages, especially the quotations, do not reflect typical sixteenth-century Buddhist scholarship or language, and they give the impression that the text as we know it today is based on an older model. It may also be a product of a Korean branch of the ancient school. The method taught in this manual is basic and quintessential in theory and practice, setting the stage for the texts that follow.

The second manual, *Models for Sitting Meditation*, was composed by Chan Buddhist Master Cijiao of Changlu in late eleventh-century China. Little is known of Cijiao, except that he was not only a master of the powerful Linji school of Chan Buddhism but also a patriarch of popular Pure Land Buddhism. The combination of Chan and Pure Land Buddhism, especially in the domain of concentration technique, is commonly found in the records of early meditation schools of China, Korea, Japan, Tibet, and Vietnam.

The next manual, *Guidelines for Sitting Meditation*, was written by Foxin Bencai, a younger contemporary of Cijiao. The instructions of Foxin and Cijiao, both quite brief, address problems of deterioration in the quality of meditation practices and prescribe simple remedies to counteract confusion and misalignment in order to foster the proper state of mind.

These two texts are followed by another short manual for general audiences, *A Generally Recommended Mode of Sitting Meditation*, by the Japanese Zen Master Dōgen. Dōgen (1200–1253) was one of the pioneers of Zen Buddhism in Japan. Scion of a distinguished and powerful family, Dōgen was originally trained as a Confucian and groomed for ministerial service in the imperial government. He also began to study Buddhism at an early age, however, and ran away from home to become a Buddhist monk, on the eve of his debut at court.

Dōgen was an intellectually brilliant individual and mastered the theories of the exoteric and esoteric branches of the old Tendai school of Japanese Buddhism in a comparatively short time. Even before his Tendai studies were over, Dōgen began to look into Zen, newly imported from continental China. Eventually he came to concentrate on Zen, and even though he was locally recognized as a master at an early age, Dōgen decided to cross over into China to study Chan, the precursor of Zen, as it was then being practiced on the continent.

After five years in China, Dōgen returned to Japan with a more complete understanding of Zen than he had been able to acquire earlier. He spent nearly ten more years observing the situation in Japan before beginning to teach. One of the main concerns of Dōgen's teaching activity was to alert people to the shortcomings and dangers of incomplete Zen meditation and partial Zen experience. This manual, one of Dōgen's first written works, reflects this concern and outlines an approach to its resolution.

The next manual presented here, *Secrets of Cultivating the Mind*, was composed by Chinul (1158–1210), founder of the Chogye order of Korean Buddhism. Ordained as a monk at the age of eight, Chinul had no teacher. His first awakening occurred as he read a Chan Buddhist classic when he was twenty-five years old. After that, Chinul went into seclusion in the mountains. Later on, he perused the whole Buddhist canon, then went back into solitude in a mountain fastness. During this period, Chinul experienced another awakening while reading the letters of one of the great Chinese masters.

Eventually Chinul began to instruct others, establishing a number of teaching centers. He attracted the attention of the Buddhist king of Koryo Korea and was honored with the title National Teacher after his passing. Based on classical teachings, Chinul's *Secrets of Cultivating the Mind* is a highly accessible primer of basic Buddhist meditation, defining and contrasting the principles and methods of sudden and gradual enlightenment.

The next manual translated here, *Absorption in the Treasury of Light*, was written by the Japanese Zen Master Ejō (1198–1282). Born into an ancient noble family, Ejō became a Buddhist monk at the age of eighteen. After studying Tendai Buddhism, Ejō concentrated on Pure Land Buddhism, then turned to Zen. Eventually he became an apprentice of Zen master Dōgen, who soon appointed Ejō his teaching assistant and spiritual successor.

Most of Ejō's later life was devoted to perpetuating the works of his teacher Dōgen, whom he survived by thirty years. The unusual *Absorption in the Treasury of Light* is Ejō's own composition. Reflecting Ejō's background in the esoteric branch of Tendai Buddhism as well as his classical Zen studies, this work shows how to focus on the so-called Dharmakāya, or Reality Body teaching of Buddhism, underlying a wide variety of symbolic expressions. This type of meditation, using scriptural extracts, poetry, and Zen koans, or teaching stories, to register a specific level of consciousness, is called *sanzen*. There is a great deal of Zen literature deriving from centuries of *sanzen*, among which

Ejō's *Absorption in the Treasury of Light* represents a very unusual blend of complexity and simplicity, depth and accessibility.

The last meditation manual, *An Elementary Talk on Zen*, is attributed to Man-an, an old adept of a Sōtō school of Zen who is believed to have lived in the early seventeenth century. The Sōtō schools of Zen in that time traced their spiritual lineages back to Dōgen and Ejō, but their doctrines and methods were not quite the same as the ancient masters', reflecting later accretions from other schools.

Man-an's work is very accessible and extremely interesting for the range of its content. In particular, it reflects a modern trend toward emphasis on meditation in action, which can be seen in China particularly from the eleventh century, in Korea from the twelfth century, and in Japan from the fourteenth century.

A few years ago, the central authority of the Roman Catholic Church issued a statement about meditation, warning that altered mental and physical states could be mistaken by the unwary for authentic spiritual experiences. Although this statement provoked a negative reaction from certain meditation groups, the fact is that the same warning is traditional in authentic Buddhism.

The fact that many Westerners have been left confused and even mentally and physically injured by supposed Eastern meditation methods is not because they were not good Catholics but because they failed to observe all the requirements of traditional meditation science. The psychopathology of meditative malpractice is well known and thoroughly described in Buddhist literature, but certain cults regularly plunge people into intensive meditation without sufficient background knowledge, understanding, and experience. Sometimes this is not done out of sheer ignorance but as a calculated recruitment tool, because people become extremely vulnerable to fixation and conditioning under these circumstances.

It was for this reason that the Tibetan Gelugpa, or Virtuous school, whose head is the Dalai Lama, reformed the practice of meditation to prevent such abuses. In that school the practitioner is expected to become thoroughly familiar with the science of meditation before plunging into intense concentration. The Chan-Taoist Master Liu I-ming similarly encouraged people to study for ten years before starting intensive meditation. The early modern Japanese Zen master Kōsen prescribed a course of study requiring about three years before he allowed students to participate in concentrated Zen work with a teacher.

Preparatory study is also useful for recognition and evaluation of teachers, an issue of serious concern to Westerners. If you go to a real teacher unprepared, you will be wasting the teacher's time and unconsciously demonstrating your own greed and laziness as well; if you go to a false teacher unprepared, you will be wasting your own time and putting yourself and your dependents in danger besides. Hence the classical Chan saying, "First awaken on your own, then see someone else." That is the purpose for which the instruction manuals presented in this book were originally composed and published.

CHAN MASTER HONGREN (602-675)

Treatise on the Supreme Vehicle

In aiming for the enlightenment of sages to understand the   1
true source, if the essential issue of cultivating the mind is
not kept pure, there is no way for any practice to yield
realization. If any good friends copy this text, be careful
not to omit anything, lest you cause people of later times
to err.

The basic essence of cultivating enlightenment should be   2
discerned: it is the inherently complete and pure mind, in
which there is no false discrimination, and body and mind
are fundamentally pure, unborn, and undying. This is the
basic teacher; this is better than invoking the Buddhas of
the ten directions.

Question: How do we know that the inherent mind is   3
fundamentally pure?

Answer: According to *The Ten Stages Scripture*, there is an
indestructible Buddha-nature in the bodies of living beings,
like the orb of the sun, its body luminous, round and full,
vast and boundless; but because it is covered by the dark
clouds of the five clusters, it cannot shine, like a lamp
inside a pitcher.

When there are clouds and fog everywhere, the world is
dark, but that does not mean the sun has decomposed.
Why is there no light? The light is never destroyed; it is

just enshrouded by clouds and fog. The pure mind of all living beings is like this, merely covered up by the dark clouds of obsession with objects, arbitrary thoughts, psychological afflictions, and views and opinions. If you can just keep the mind still so that errant thought does not arise, the reality of nirvana will naturally appear. This is how we know the inherent mind is originally pure.

4   Question: How do we know the inherent mind is fundamentally unborn and undying?

Answer: *The Scripture Spoken by Vimalakīrti* says that suchness has no birth and suchness has no death. Suchness is true thusness, the Buddha-nature that is inherently pure. Purity is the source of mind; true thusness is always there and does not arise from conditions.

The scripture also says that all ordinary beings are *thus*, and all sages and saints are also *thus*. "All ordinary beings" refers to us; "all sages and saints" refers to the Buddhas. Although their names and appearances differ, the objective nature of true thusness in their bodies is the same. Being unborn and undying, it is called *thus*. This is how we know the inherent mind is fundamentally unborn and undying.

5   Question: Why call the inherent mind the basic teacher?

Answer: This true mind is natural and does not come from outside. It is not confined to cultivation in past, present, or future. The dearest and most intimate thing there could be is to preserve the mind yourself. If you know the mind, you will reach transcendence by preserving it. If you are confused about the mind and ignore it, you will fall into miserable states. Thus we know that the Buddhas of all times consider the inherent mind to be the basic teacher. Therefore a treatise says, "Preserve the mind with perfect clarity so that errant thoughts do not arise, and this is birthlessness." This is how we know the mind is the basic teacher.

Question: What does it mean to say that the inherent 6 mind is better than invoking other Buddhas?

Answer: Even if you constantly invoke other Buddhas, you will not escape birth and death; but if you preserve your own basic mind, you will arrive at transcendence. *The Diamond Cutter Scripture* says that anyone who views Buddha in terms of form or seeks Buddha through sound is traveling an aberrant path and cannot see the real Buddha. Therefore it is said that preserving the true mind is better than invoking other Buddhas.

The word *better*, nevertheless, is only used to encourage people. In reality, the essence of the ultimate realization is equal, without duality.

Question: Since the true essence of Buddhas and ordinary 7 beings is the same, why do Buddhas experience infinite happiness and unhindered freedom, without birth or death, while we ordinary beings fall into birth and death and suffer all sorts of pains?

Answer: The Buddhas of the ten directions realized the true nature of things and spontaneously perceive the source of mind; errant imagining does not arise, accurate awareness is not lost. The egoistic, possessive attitude disappears, so they are not subject to birth and death. Because they are not subject to birth and death, they are ultimately tranquil; so obviously all happiness naturally comes to them.

Ordinary people lose sight of the nature of reality and do not know the basis of mind. Arbitrarily fixating on all sorts of objects, they do not cultivate accurate awareness;

therefore love and hatred arise. Because of love and hatred, the vessel of mind cracks and leaks. Because the vessel of mind cracks and leaks, there is birth and death. Because there is birth and death, all miseries naturally appear.

The Mind King Scripture says that true thusness, the Buddha-nature, is submerged in the ocean of cognition, perception, and sense, bobbing up and down in birth and death, unable to escape. Effort should be made to preserve the basic true mind, so that arbitrary thoughts do not arise, egoistic and possessive attitudes vanish, and you spontaneously realize equality and unity with the Buddhas.

8   Question: If the Buddha-nature that is truly *thus* is one and the same, then when one is deluded, everyone should be deluded, and when one is enlightened, everyone should be enlightened. Why is it that when Buddhas awaken to this nature, the ignorance and confusion of ordinary people remain the same?

Answer: From here on, we enter the domain of the inconceivable, beyond the reach of ordinary people. Enlightenment is realized by knowing mind; confusion happens because of losing touch with nature. If conditions meet, they meet; no fixed statement can be made. Just trust in the truth and preserve your inherent basic mind.

This is why *The Scripture Spoken by Vimalakīrti* says that there is neither selfhood nor otherness, that reality has never been born and does not presently perish. This is realizing the dualistic extremism of identification and alienation, thus entering into nondiscriminatory knowledge. If you understand this point, then preserving the mind is foremost among the essentials of the teachings on practical knowledge. This practice of preserving the mind is the basis of nirvana, the essential doorway into enlightenment, the source of all the scriptures, and the progenitor of the Buddhas of all times.

Question: How do we know that preserving the fundamental true mind is the basis of nirvana? 9

Answer: The essence of nirvana is tranquil, uncontrived bliss. Realize your own mind is the true mind, and errant imagining ceases. When errant imagining ceases, you are accurately aware. By virtue of accurate awareness, dispassionately perceptive knowledge arises. By dispassionately perceptive knowledge, one finds out the nature of reality. By finding out the nature of reality, one attains nirvana. This is how we know that preserving the fundamental true mind is the basis of nirvana.

Question: How do we know that preserving the fundamental true mind is the essential doorway into enlightenment? 10

Answer: "Even if you draw a figure of a Buddha with your finger, or perform countless virtuous deeds . . ."—teachings like this are just Buddha's instructions for ignorant people to create causes for better future states, and even for seeing Buddha. As for those who wish to attain Buddhahood quickly on their own, they should preserve the basic true mind. The Buddhas of past, present, and future are infinite, but not one of them attained Buddhahood without preserving the basic true mind. Therefore a scripture says that if you keep the mind on one point, there is nothing that cannot be accomplished. This is how we know that preserving the basic true mind is the essential doorway into enlightenment.

11   Question: How do we know that preserving the basic true mind is the source of all the scriptures?

Answer: In the scriptures, the Buddha explains all the causes and conditions, results and consequences, of all sins and virtues, drawing upon even the mountains, rivers, earth, grasses, trees, and other beings for countless parables, similes, and metaphors, on occasion manifesting countless varieties of spiritual powers and emanations. This is all because Buddha teaches people who lack insight but have all sorts of desires and innumerable different mentalities.

On this account, the Buddha uses means suited to individual mentalities in order to lead people into universal truth. Once we know that the Buddha-nature in all beings is as pure as the sun behind the clouds, if we just preserve the basic true mind with perfect clarity, the clouds of errant thoughts will come to an end, and the sun of insight will emerge; what is the need for so much more study of knowledge of the pains of birth and death, of all sorts of doctrines and principles, and of the affairs of past, present, and future? It is like wiping the dust off a mirror; the clarity appears spontaneously when the dust is all gone.

Thus whatever is learned in the present unenlightened mind is worthless. If you can maintain accurate awareness clearly, what you learn in the uncontrived mind is true learning.

But even though I call it real learning, ultimately there is nothing learned. Why? Because both the self and nirvana are empty; there is no more two, not even one. Thus there is nothing learned; but even though phenomena are essentially empty, it is necessary to preserve the basic true

6

mind with perfect clarity, because then delusive thoughts do not arise, and egoism and possessiveness disappear. *The Nirvana Scripture* says, "Those who know the Buddha does not preach anything are called fully learned." This is how we know that preserving the basic true mind is the source of all the scriptures.

Question: How do we know that preserving the basic 12 true mind is the progenitor of the Buddhas of all times?

Answer: The Buddhas of all times are born from the essence of mind. First preserve the true mind so that errant thoughts do not arise; then, after egoism and possessiveness have vanished, you can attain Buddhahood.

The foregoing dialogues could be expanded endlessly; 13 my hope for now is that you will become conscious that your own basic mind is Buddha. This is why I exhort you so earnestly; nothing in the thousands of scriptures and myriads of treatises surpasses preserving the basic true mind—this is essential.

Now I will make further effort to instruct you by refer- 14 ence to *The Lotus of Truth Scripture*'s symbols of the great chariot, the treasure trove, the bright pearl, the wondrous herb: it's just that you yourself do not take and use them; that is why you suffer misery.

What should you do? When errant thoughts do not arise, 15 and egoism and possessiveness disappear, then all virtuous qualities come to fulfillment naturally; you need not seek externally, for that brings you back to the miseries of birth and death. Wherever you are, examine your mind with accurate awareness. Do not plant seeds of future misery by attachment to present pleasure, fooling yourself and deceiving others, not getting free of birth and death.

16   Work, work! Although the present is transitory, together make the basis of future Buddhahood. Do not let past, present, and future go to waste, uselessly killing time. A scripture speaks of "being in hell as though it were a pleasure garden" and "being in other bad states as though in your own house." That we ordinary mortals are presently like this unconsciously amazes people totally, but nothing is beyond mind. How wonderful! How miserable!

17   If there are beginners learning to sit and meditate, follow the directions in *The Scripture on Visualization of Infinite Life*: sit straight, accurately aware, with eyes closed and mouth shut. Mentally gaze evenly before you, as near or far as you wish: visualize the sun, preserving the true mind, keeping your attention on this uninterruptedly. Then tune your breathing, not letting it fluctuate between coarseness and fineness, for that causes illness and pain.

18   When you sit and meditate at night, you may see all sorts of scenes, good and bad. Or you may become totally absorbed in blue, yellow, red, white, and so on. You may perceive your body radiating tremendous light, you may see the form of a Buddha, or you may see all sorts of miraculous productions. Just know enough to collect your mind and not be attached to any of that, for all of it is empty, seen only because of subjective imagination. A scripture says, "All lands in the ten directions are like space; all worlds are illusory, just construed by mind."

19   If you do not enter trance and do not see all sorts of visions, do not wonder; just keep the basic true mind perfectly clear at all times, whatever you are doing, so that errant thoughts do not arise and egoism and possessiveness disappear.

Nothing is outside the inherent mind; the Buddhas expounded so many doctrines and parables because the patterns of ordinary people's behaviors are not the same. Eventually this caused the frameworks of the teaching to differ, but in reality the substance of the states of the eighty-four thousand doctrines, the three vehicles, and the eightfold path, the source of the seventy-two grades of illuminates, are not beyond the inherent mind, which is the basis. If you know the basic mind firsthand and continue to polish it moment to moment, then you will naturally see the Buddha-nature; at every moment you will be presenting offerings to countless Buddhas of the ten directions, while all the scriptures of the canon will be "recited" in every moment. 20

If you comprehend the mind source, then all meaningful mental phenomena spontaneously appear, all vows come to fulfillment, all practices are completed. Everything is done; you are no longer subject to becoming. It is necessary that errant thoughts do not arise and egoism and possessiveness disappear; after you relinquish this body, you will certainly attain the uncreate, the inconceivable. 21

Work! Don't waste a moment. Words as true and undeceptive as these are hard to get to hear; those who hear them and actually put them into practice are extremely rare, and those who practice and actually attain them are even more rare. 22

Calm yourself, quiet yourself, master your senses. Look right into the source of mind, always keep it shining bright, clear and pure. Do not give rise to an indifferent mind. 23

Question: What do you mean by an indifferent mind? 24

Answer: When people who concentrate their minds focus

on external objects, and their coarse mentalities cease for a while because of it, they inwardly refine the true mind; when the mind is not yet pure and clear, and they examine the mind constantly, whatever they are doing, and yet are unable to clearly perceive the mind source independently, this is called an indifferent mind.

This is still a contaminated mind, which does not as yet escape the great illness of birth and death. How about those who don't preserve the true mind at all! Such people sink into the bitter sea of birth and death; when will they ever get out? What a pity! Work, work!

Scripture says that if people's true sincerity does not emerge from within, even if they meet countless Buddhas past, present, and future, they can do nothing. Scripture also says that when people know the mind, they liberate themselves; Buddhas cannot liberate people. If Buddhas could liberate people, why have people like us not attained enlightenment in spite of the fact that there have been countless Buddhas in the past? It is just that true sincerity does not come from within; therefore people sink in a sea of bitterness.

Work, work! Diligently seek the basic mind; do not allow random contamination. What is past is not our concern; we cannot catch up with what has already gone by. I urge those who have now, in the present, gotten to hear the subtle teaching, to understand these words: realize that preserving the mind is the foremost path.

25   If you are unwilling to exercise utmost sincerity in the quest for enlightenment and its experience of infinite freedom and happiness, and instead start making a lot of noise, following the mundane, greedily seeking honor and profit,

you will fall into a vast hell and suffer all kinds of misery. What can you do about this? How will you manage? What will you do?

Work, work! Just dress in old clothes, eat simple food, 26 and preserve the basic true mind with perfect clarity. Feign ignorance, appear inarticulate. This is most economical with energy, yet effective. This is characteristic of very diligent people.

Deluded worldly people who do not understand this 27 principle undertake many hardships in ignorance to carry out apparent good on a large scale. They hope to attain liberation, but return to birth and death. As for those who maintain accurate awareness with perfect clarity and liberate other people, they are powerful enlightening beings.

I tell you all clearly, preserving the mind is number one; 28 if you do not make any effort to preserve the mind, you are extremely foolish. By not accepting the present, you suffer a lifetime of misery; by wishing for the future, you suffer calamity for myriad aeons. If I indulge you, I don't know what more I can tell you.

The one who is unmoved by the blowing of the eight 29 winds is the real mountain of jewels. One who knows the result just acts and speaks with skillful fluidity to adapt to all situations, giving out remedies in accordance with illnesses; one who can do this and yet not conceive false thoughts, so that egoism and possessiveness are extinct, has truly transcended the world.

When the Buddha was alive, he had no end of praise for 30 this; I speak of it to encourage you earnestly. If you do not create false ideas and are void of egoism and possessiveness, then you are beyond the world.

11

31   Question: What is the disappearance of egoism and possessiveness?

Answer: If you have any desire to surpass others, or any thought of your own ability, this is egoism and possessiveness. These are sicknesses in the context of nirvana, so *The Nirvana Scripture* says, "Space can contain everything, but space does not entertain the thought that it can contain everything." This is a metaphor for the disappearance of egoism and possessiveness, by which you proceed to indestructible concentration.

32   Question: Practitioners seeking true eternal peace who care only for the transient crude virtues of the world and do not care for the truly eternal subtle virtues of ultimate truth have not seen the principle, and just want to arouse their minds to focus on doctrines to pursue in thought; as soon as conscious awareness occurs, it is contaminated. But if one wants only to forget the mind, this is the darkness of ignorance; it is not in accord with true principle. If one just wants to neither stop the mind nor focus on principles, this is wrongly grasping emptiness, living like an animal in spite of being human. At such times, if one has no methods of concentration and insight and cannot understand how to see the Buddha-nature clearly, the practitioner will only get bogged down—how can one transcend this to arrive at complete nirvana? Please point out the true mind.

Answer: You need to have complete confidence and effective determination. Gently quiet your mind, and I will instruct you again.

You should make your own body and mind unfettered and serene, not entangled in any objects at all. Sit straight, accurately aware, and tune your breathing so that it is properly adjusted. Examine your mind to see it as not being inside, not being outside, and not being in between. Observe it calmly, carefully, and objectively; when you master this, you will clearly see that the mind's consciousness moves in a flow, like a current of water, like heat waves rising endlessly.

When you have seen this consciousness, you find it is neither inside nor outside: unhurriedly, objectively, calmly observe. When you master this, then melt and flux over and over, empty yet solid, profoundly stable, and then this flowing consciousness will vanish.

Those who get this consciousness to vanish thereby destroy the obstructing confusions of the enlightening beings of the ten stages. Once this consciousness has vanished, then the mind is open and still, silent, serene and calm, immaculately pure, and tremendously steady.

I cannot explain this state any further. If you want to attain it, take up the chapter in *The Nirvana Scripture* on the indestructible body, and the chapter in *The Scripture Spoken by Vimalakīrti* on seeing the Immovable Buddha: contemplate and reflect on them unhurriedly, search them carefully and read them thoroughly. If you are completely familiar with these scriptures and can actually maintain this mind whatever you are doing, in the face of the five desires and eight winds, then your pure conduct is established and your task is done; in the end you will not be subjected to a body that is born and dies.

The five desires are desires for form, sound, fragrance, flavor, and feeling. The eight winds are profit and loss, censure and praise, respect and ridicule, pain and pleasure. This is where practitioners polish and refine the Buddha-nature; it's no wonder if one does not attain independence in this body. Scripture says, "If there is nowhere for a Buddha to sojourn in the world, enlightening beings cannot actually function."

If you want to be free of this conditional body, do not discriminate between the past sharpness or dullness of human faculties; the best require but a moment, the least take countless aeons.

33 If you have the strength and the time to develop altruistic roots of virtues according to people's natures, thus to help yourself and others as well, adorning a Buddha-land, you must understand the Four Reliances and find out what reality is actually like. If you rely on clinging to the letter, you will lose the true source.

34 For mendicants learning to study the Way as renunciants, the fact is that "leaving home" means getting out of the fetters of birth and death: that is called "leaving home."

When accurate mindfulness is completely present and cultivation of the Way is successful, even if you are dismembered, as long as you do not lose right mindfulness at the moment of death, you will immediately attain Buddhahood.

35 I have composed the foregoing treatise simply by taking the sense of scriptures according to faith; in reality, I do not know by perfectly complete experience. If there is anything contrary to the Buddha's principles, I will willingly repent and eliminate it; whatever is in accord with the Buddha's path, I donate to all beings, hoping that everyone will get to know the basic mind and attain enlightenment at once. May those who hear this work become Buddhas in the future; I hope you will liberate my followers first.

36 Question: From beginning to end, everything in this

14

treatise reveals that the inherent mind is the Way; does it belong to the category of actualization, or to the category of practice?

Answer: The heart of this treatise is to reveal the One Vehicle. Its ultimate intent, therefore, is to guide the deluded so that they may extricate themselves from birth and death; only then can they liberate others. Speaking only of self-help and not of helping others is characteristic of the category of practice; whoever practices in accord with the text will be the first to attain Buddhahood. If I am deceiving you, in the future I will fall into eighteen hells. I promise to heaven and earth: if I am not being truthful, let me be devoured by tigers and wolves lifetime after lifetime.

late 11 century

CHAN MASTER CIJIAO
OF CHANGLU

Models for
Sitting Meditation

1   Those who aspire to enlightenment and who would learn wisdom should first arouse an attitude of great compassion and make an all-encompassing vow to master concentration, promising to liberate other people, not seeking liberation for your own self alone.

2   Then and only then should you let go of all objects and put to rest all concerns, so that body and mind are one suchness, and there is no gap between movement and stillness.

3   Moderate your food and drink, taking neither too much nor too little. Regulate your sleep, neither restricting it too much nor indulging in it too much.

4   When you are going to sit in meditation, spread a thick sitting mat in a quiet, uncluttered place. Wear your clothing loosely, but maintain uniform order in your posture and carriage.

5   Then sit in the lotus posture, first placing the right foot on the left thigh, then placing the left foot on the right thigh. The half-lotus posture will also do; just put the left foot on the right leg, that is all.

6   Next, place the right hand on the left ankle, and place the left hand, palm up, on the palm of the right hand. Have the thumbs of both hands brace each other up.

Slowly raise the body forward, and also rock to the left 7
and right, then sit straight. Do not lean to the left or right,
do not tilt forward or backward. Align the joints of your
hips, your spine, and the base of the skull so that they
support each other, your form like a stupa. Yet you should
not make your body too extremely erect, for that constricts
the breathing and makes it uncomfortable. The ears should
be aligned with the shoulders, the nose with the navel.
The tongue rests on the upper palate, the lips and teeth
are touching.

The eyes should be slightly open, to avoid bringing on 8
oblivion and drowsiness. If you are going to attain meditation concentration, that power is supreme. In ancient times
there were eminent monks specializing in concentration
practice who always kept their eyes open when they sat.
Chan Master Fayun Yuantong also scolded people for
sitting in meditation with their eyes closed, calling it a
ghost cave in a mountain of darkness. Evidently there is
deep meaning in this, of which adepts are aware.

Once the physical posture is settled and the breath is 9
tuned, then relax your lower abdomen. Do not think of
anything good or bad. When a thought arises, notice it;
when you become aware of it, it disappears. Eventually you
forget mental objects and spontaneously become unified.
This is the essential art of sitting Zen meditation.

In spite of the fact that sitting Zen meditation is a 10
scientific way to peace and bliss, many people do it in a
pathological manner that brings on sickness. This is because
they do not apply their minds correctly. If you get the true
sense, then your body will naturally feel light and easy,
while your vital spirit will be clear and keen. True mindful-

ness is distinctly clear, the savor of truth sustains the spirit, and you experience pure bliss in a state of profound serenity.

11   For those who have already had an awakening, this can be said to be like a dragon finding water, like a tiger in the mountains. For those who have not yet had an awakening, it is still using the wind to blow on the fire; the effort required is not much. Just make the mind receptive and you will not be cheated.

12   Nevertheless, when the Way is lofty, demons abound; all sorts of things offend and please. As long as you keep true mindfulness present, however, none of this can hold you back.

13   The *Shūrangama-sūtra*, the Tiantai manuals of "stopping and seeing," and Guifeng's *Guidelines for Cultivation and Realization* fully explains bedevilments. Those whose preparation is insufficient should not fail to know these.

14   When you want to come out of concentration, slowly rock the body and rise calmly and carefully, avoiding haste.

15   After coming out of concentration, at all times use whatever means expedient to preserve the power of concentration, as if you were taking care of a baby. Then the power of concentration will be easy to perfect.

16   Meditation concentration is a most urgent task. If you do not meditate calmly and reflect quietly, you will be utterly at a loss in this domain. So if you are going to look for a pearl, it is best to still the waves; it will be hard to find if you stir the water. When the water of concentration is still and clear, the pearl of mind reveals itself.

17   Therefore *The Scripture of Complete Awakening* says, "Unhindered pure wisdom all comes from meditation concentra-

tion." *The Lotus Scripture* says, "In an unoccupied space, practice collecting the mind, stabilizing it so that it is as immovable as the Polar Mountain." So we know that in order to transcend the ordinary and go beyond the holy, one must make use of quiet meditation; to die sitting or pass away standing, one must depend on the power of concentration.

Even if you work on it all your life, you still may not 18 succeed; how much the more so if you waste time! What will you use to counteract karma? This is why the ancients said that if one lacks the power of concentration one willingly submits to death, living out one's life in vain, unseeing, like a wandering vagrant.

I hope that companions in meditation will read this tract 19 over and over, to help themselves and help others alike to attain true awakening.

CHAN MASTER FOXIN BENCAI

Guidelines for
Sitting Meditation

1 In sitting meditation, make the heart upright and the mind straight and true. Purify the self and empty the heart. Sitting cross-legged, look and listen inward; clearly awake and aware, you are permanently removed from oblivion and excitement. If something comes to mind, do your best to cast it away.

2 In quiet concentration, examine clearly with true mindfulness. What is cognizant of sitting is mind, and what introspects is mind. What knows being and nonbeing, center and extremes, inside and outside, is mind. This mind is empty yet perceptive, silent yet aware. Round and bright, perfectly clear, it does not fall into ideas of annihilation or eternity. Spiritual awareness radiantly bright, its discrimination is not false.

3 Nowadays we see students who sit diligently but do not awaken. Their problem derives from their dependence on conceptions, their feelings sticking to bias and falsehood. In their confusion they turn their backs on the true basis and mistakenly go along with quietism or activism. This is why they fail to attain enlightenment.

4 If you can concentrate and clarify your mind such that you harmonize intimately with the uncreate, the mirror of knowledge will be cleared and the flower of mind will

suddenly burst into bloom. Infinite attachments to conceptions will directly melt away, and accumulated aeons of ignorance will open up all at once.

This is like forgetting, then suddenly remembering; like 5 being sick, then all at once recovering. A sense of joy arises within, and you know you will become a Buddha. Then you know that there is no separate Buddha outside of mind.

After that you increase cultivation in accord with enlight- 6 enment, experiencing realization by cultivation. The source of realization of enlightenment is the identity of mind, Buddha, and living beings. This is called absorption in unified understanding and unified action. It is also called the effortless path.

Now you can turn things around without alienation from 7 senses and objects. Picking up what comes to hand, you alternate as host and guest. The eye of the universe clear, present and past are renewed. The spiritual capacity of direct perception is naturally attained. This is why Vimala-kīrti said, "To live an active life without emerging from absorption in extinction is called quiet sitting."

So we should know that the moon appears when the 8 water is still, the shine is complete when the mirror is clean. For people who study the Way, it is essential to sit and meditate. Otherwise, you will be going around in circles forever.

Although this is unpleasant, I cannot keep silent. I have 9 written some generalities to help people discover the true source. If you do not neglect practice, then you will attain the same realization.

ZEN MASTER DŌGEN (1200–1253)

A Generally Recommended Mode of Sitting Meditation

1 The Way is fundamentally complete and perfect, all-pervasive; how could it depend upon cultivation and realization?

2 The vehicle of the source is free; why expend effort?

3 The whole being is utterly beyond defiling dust; who would believe in a method of wiping it clean?

4 The great whole is not apart from here; why go someplace to practice?

5 Nevertheless, the slightest discrepancy is as the distance between sky and earth: as soon as aversion and attraction arise, you lose your mind in confusion.

6 Even though you may boast of comprehension and wallow in understanding, having gotten a glimpse of insight, and though you find the Way and understand the mind, inspired with the determination to soar to the skies, although you may roam freely within the bounds of initial entry, you are still somewhat lacking in a living road of emancipation.

7 Even Gautama Buddha, who had innate knowledge, sat upright for six years; this is a noteworthy example. When referring to the transmission of the mind seal at Shaolin, the fame of nine years facing a wall is still mentioned. Since the ancients did so, why should people today not do so?

8 Therefore you should stop the intellectual activity of

pursuing words and chasing sayings, and should learn the stepping back of turning the light around and looking back. Body and mind will naturally be shed, and the original countenance will become manifest.

If you want to attain something, you should set right 9 about working on it. For intensive Zen meditation, a quiet room is appropriate. Food and drink are to be moderate. Letting go of all mental objects, taking a respite from all concerns, not thinking of good or evil, not being concerned with right or wrong, halt the operations of mind, intellect, and consciousness, stop assessment by thought, imagination, and view. Do not aim to become a Buddha; and how could it be limited to sitting or reclining?

Spread a thick sitting mat where you usually sit, and use 10 a cushion on top of this. You may sit in the full-lotus posture, or in the half-lotus posture. For the full-lotus posture, first place the right foot on the left thigh, then the left foot on the right thigh. For the half-lotus posture, just place the left foot on the right thigh. Wear loose clothing, and keep it orderly.

Next place the right hand on the left leg, and the left 11 hand on the right hand, with palms facing upward. The two thumbs face each other and hold each other up.

Now sit upright, with your body straight. Do not lean to 12 the left or tilt to the right, bend forward or lean backward. Align the ears with the shoulders, and the nose with the navel. The tongue should rest on the upper palate, the teeth and lips should be closed. The eyes should always be open. The breathing passes subtly through the nose.

Once the physical form is in order, exhale fully through 13

23

the mouth once, sway left and right, then settle into sitting perfectly still.

14 Think of what does not think. How do you think of what does not think? It is not thinking.

15 This is the essential art of sitting Zen meditation.

16 What I call sitting Zen meditation is not practice of *dhyāna*. It is just a method of comfort, a practical way of experiencing thoroughgoing investigation of enlightenment: objective reality becomes manifest, beyond any trap.

17 If you can get the meaning of this, you will be like dragons taking to the water, like tigers in the mountains. You will know that the truth has spontaneously become evident, while oblivion and distraction will already have been overcome.

18 When you are going to rise from sitting, move your body gradually, getting up gently. Do not be hasty or careless.

19 We have seen stories of transcending the ordinary and going beyond the holy, shedding the mortal coil while sitting or passing away while standing upright: all of these depend on the power in this.

20 And how about the transformations of state upon the lifting of a finger, a pole, a needle, a hammer? How about the realizations of accord on the raising of a whisk, a fist, a cane, a shout? These have never been susceptible to understanding by thought and conceptualization; how could they be known by cultivated realization of supernatural powers?

21 It could be called dignified behavior beyond sound and form; is it not a guiding example prior to knowledge and views? Being such, it is not an issue whether one has more or less intelligence, making no distinction between the

24

quick and the slow. Focused, unified concentration is what constitutes work on the Way.

The practice and realization are spontaneously undefiled; 22 the process of heading for the aim, furthermore, is being normal.

Whatever they are, one's own world and the realms of 23 others, West and East, they equally hold the seal of Buddha, based as one on the way of the source.

Just work on sitting, remaining in an immobile state. 24 Even though it seems there are myriad differences and a thousand distinctions, just attend to intensive meditation to master the Way.

Why abandon a seat in your own house to idly roam in 25 the dusty realms of alien countries? Take a single misstep, and you blunder past what's right in front of you.

Having gotten the key of the human body, do not pass 26 time uselessly: preserve and uphold the essential potential of the Buddha Way.

Who has the folly to look forward to what lasts but a 27 moment? Add to this consideration the fact that the physical body is like a dewdrop on the grass, a lifetime is like a lightning flash: all of a sudden they are void, in an instant they are gone.

May those high-minded people who participate in this 28 study and have long learned to feel an elephant by hand not be suspicious of a real dragon. Proceed energetically on the straightforward path of direct pointing, and honor people who have transcended learning and gone beyond effort. Join in the enlightenment of the Buddhas, inherit the state of mind of the Zen founders.

Having long been thus, we should be thus. The treasury 29 opens of itself, to be used at will.

SON MASTER CHINUL (1158-1210)

Secrets of
Cultivating the Mind

1   The triple world with its irritating vexations is like a house afire; who could bear to stay there long, willingly suffering perpetual torment?

2   If you want to avoid going around in circles, nothing compares to seeking Buddhahood. If you want to seek Buddhahood, Buddha is mind. Need mind be sought afar? It is not apart from the body.

3   The material body is temporal, having birth and death. The real mind is like space, unending and unchanging. Thus it is said, "When the physical body decays and dissolves back into fire and air, one thing remains aware, encompassing the universe."

4   Unfortunately, people today have been confused for a long time. They do not know that their own mind is the real Buddha. They do not know that their own essence is the real Dharma. Wishing to seek the Dharma, they attribute it to remote sages; wishing to seek Buddhahood, they do not observe their own mind.

5   If you say that there is Buddha outside of mind, and there is Dharma outside of essence, and want to seek the Way of Buddhahood while clinging tightly to these feelings, even if you spend ages burning your body, branding your arms, breaking your bones and taking out the marrow, wounding

yourself and copying scriptures in your own blood, sitting for long periods of time without sitting down, eating only once a day, reading the whole canon and cultivating various austere practices, it will be like steaming sand to produce cooked rice; it will only increase your own fatigue.

Just know your own mind and you will grasp countless   6 teachings and infinite subtle meanings without even seeking. That is why the World Honored One said, "Observing all sentient beings, I see they are fully endowed with the knowledge and virtues of Buddhas." He also said, "All living beings, and all sorts of illusory events, are all born in the completely awake subtle mind of those who realize suchness."

So we know that there is no Buddhahood to attain apart   7 from this mind. The Realized Ones of the past were just people who understood the mind, and the saints and sages of the present are people who cultivate the mind; students of the future should rely on this principle.

People who practice the Way should not seek externally.   8 The essence of mind has no defilement; it is originally complete and perfect of itself. Just detach from illusory objects and it is enlightened to suchness as is.

Question: If Buddha-nature is presently in our bodies, it   9 is not apart from ordinary people. Then why do we not perceive Buddha-nature now?

Answer: It is in your body, but you do not perceive it   10 yourself. At all times you know when you are hungry, you know when you are thirsty, you know when you are cold, you know when you are hot; sometimes you get angry, sometimes you are joyful—ultimately, what is it that does all this?

11　　Now then, the material body is a compound of four elements: earth, water, fire, and air. Their substance is insentient; how can they perceive or cognize? That which can perceive and cognize has to be your Buddha-nature.

12　　This is why Linji said, "The four gross elements cannot expound the Teaching or listen to the Teaching. Space cannot expound the Teaching or listen to the Teaching. Only the solitary light clearly before you, that which has no form, can expound the Teaching or listen to the Teaching."

13　　What he called that which has no form is the stamp of the truth of all Buddhas, and it is your original mind. So the Buddha-nature is presently in your body; what need is there to seek outside? If you do not believe it, let me mention some stories of how ancient sages entered the Way, to enable you to clear up your doubts. You should believe with clear understanding of truth.

14　　In ancient times a king asked a Buddhist saint, "What is Buddhahood?"

The saint said, "Seeing essence is Buddhahood."

The king asked, "Do you see essence?"

The saint said, "I see the essence of enlightenment."

The king asked, "Where is essence?"

The saint said, "Essence is in function."

The king asked, "What function is this, that it is not now visible?"

The saint said, "It is now functioning; it is just that you yourself do not see it."

The king asked, "Does it exist in me?"

The saint said, "Whenever you act, that is it. When you are inactive, the essence is again hard to see."

28

The king asked, "When it is to be employed, in how many places does it appear?"

The saint said, "When it appears, there must be eight places."

The king said, "Please explain those eight manifestations."

The saint said, "In the womb, it is called the body. In society, it is called the person. In the eyes, it is called seeing. In the ears, it is called hearing. In the nose, it distinguishes scents. In the tongue, it talks. In the hands, it grabs and holds. In the feet, it walks and runs. It manifests all over, including everything; countless worlds are collected in a single atom. Perceptives know this is the Buddha-nature, the essence of enlightenment. Those who do not know call it the soul."

On hearing this, the mind of the king was opened up to understanding.

Also, a monk asked Master Guizong, "What is Buddha?" *15*

Guizong said, "If I tell you right now, I'm afraid you won't believe it."

The monk said, "If you speak truly, how dare I not believe?"

Guizong said, "You yourself are it."

The monk asked, "How can I preserve it?"

Guizong said, "When there is a single obstruction in the eye, there is a shower of flowers in the sky."

That monk attained insight at these words.

These stories I have quoted about the circumstances of *16* ancient sages' entry into the Way are clear and simple. They certainly save energy. If you gain true understanding by these stories, then you walk hand in hand with the ancient sages.

17   Question: You speak of seeing essence. Those who have really seen essence are then sages. As such, they should be different from other people, manifesting spiritual powers and miracles. Why is there not a single practitioner today manifesting spiritual powers and miracles?

18   Answer: You shouldn't be too quick to speak wild words. Those who do not distinguish the false from the true are confused and deluded people. Students of the Way today talk about truth, but in their hearts they get bored and fall back into the error of being indiscriminate—these are the ones you doubt. To study the Way without knowing what goes before and what comes later, to speak of principle without distinguishing root and branch, is called false opinion, not cultivation of learning. You not only cause yourself to go wrong, you also cause others to go wrong. Should you not be careful?

19   There are many avenues of entry into the Way, but essentially they all fall within the two categories of sudden enlightenment and gradual practice. Even though we speak of sudden enlightenment and immediate practice, this is how those of the very highest faculties and potential gain entry; and if you look into their past, they have already practiced gradual cultivation based on sudden enlightenment for many lifetimes, so that in the present life they realize enlightenment immediately upon hearing the truth, suddenly finished all at once. In reality, these people are also included in the category of those who are first enlightened and then practice.

20   So these two aspects, sudden and gradual, are the guide-

lines followed by all sages. Sages since time immemorial have all first awakened and then cultivated practice, attaining experiential proof based on practice. So-called spiritual powers and miracles are manifested by the gradual cultivation of practice based on enlightenment; it is not that they appear immediately upon enlightenment. As scripture says, "The abstract principle is understood all of a sudden; concrete matters are cleared up by means of this understanding. They are not cleared away all at once but worked through in an orderly manner."

This is why Guifeng said, in a profound explanation of 21 the meaning of first awakening and then cultivating practice, "Consciousness is an ice pond: though it is all water, it needs the energy of the sun to melt. When ordinary people are awakened, they are Buddhas; but they rely on the power of the Dharma for cultivation. When ice melts, then water flows and moistens; only then can it perform its irrigating function. When delusion is ended, then the mind is open and penetrating, responsively manifesting the function of the light of spiritual powers."

So factual spiritual powers and miracles cannot be accom- 22 plished in one day; they appear after gradual cultivation. And what is more, from the point of view of those who have arrived, concrete supernatural powers are still apparitional affairs, and they are minor things to sages; even if they manifest, it is not right to want to use them.

Confused and ignorant people today imagine that count- 23 less subtle functions, spiritual powers, and miracles will immediately appear upon an instantaneous awakening. If you entertain this understanding, this means you do not know what comes first and what follows afterward, and cannot distinguish the root from the branches. If you try to seek enlightenment without knowing what comes first and what follows afterward, what is basic and what is derivative, that is like trying to put a square peg in a round hole. Is it not a big mistake?

24 Since you do not know expedient technique, you imagine you are facing a sheer precipice, and thus lose interest. Many are those who cut off their potential for enlightenment in this way. Since they themselves have not attained enlightenment, they do not believe that others have realized any enlightenment. Seeing those without spiritual powers, they become contemptuous and make the sages and saints out to be cheaters and deceivers. This is pitiful indeed.

25 Question: You say that the two categories of sudden enlightenment and gradual practice are guidelines followed by all sages. If enlightenment is sudden enlightenment, what is the need for gradual practice? If practice is gradual practice, why speak of sudden enlightenment? Please explain the meanings of sudden and gradual further, to eliminate remaining doubts.

26 Answer: As for sudden enlightenment, as long as ordinary people are deluded, they think their bodies are material conglomerates and their minds are random thoughts. They do not know that inherent essence is the true body of reality. They do not know that their own open awareness is the real Buddha. Seeking Buddha outside of mind, they run randomly from one impulse to another.

27 If a real teacher points out a way of entry for you, and for a single instant you turn your attention around, you see your own original essence. This essence originally has no

32

afflictions; uncontaminated wisdom is inherently complete in it. Then you are no different from the Buddhas; thus it is called sudden enlightenment.

As for gradual practice, having suddenly realized funda-   28
mental essence, no different from Buddha, beginningless mental habits are hard to get rid of all at once. Therefore one cultivates practice based on enlightenment, gradually cultivating the attainment to perfection, nurturing the embryo of sagehood to maturity. Eventually, after a long time, one becomes a sage; therefore it is called gradual practice. It is like an infant, which has all the normal faculties at birth, but as yet undeveloped; only with the passage of years does it become an adult.

Question: By what expedient means can we turn our   29
minds around instantly to realize our inherent essence?

Answer: It is just your own mind; what further expedient   30
means would you apply? If you apply expedient means to go on to seek intellectual understanding, this is like wanting to see your own eyes because you think you have no eyes if you cannot see them. Since they are your own eyes, how can you see them? As long as you have not lost them, that is called seeing eyes. If you have no more desire to see, does that mean you imagine you are not seeing? So it is also with one's own open awareness. Since it is one's own mind, how can one yet seek to see it? If you seek understanding, then you do not understand it. Just know that which does not understand; this is seeing essence.

Question: The most superior people easily understand   31
upon hearing; middling and lesser people are not without doubt. Please give further explanations of means to enable confused people to gain direction and access.

33

32   Answer: The Way is not in the province of knowing or not knowing. Get rid of the mind that uses confusion to anticipate enlightenment, and listen to what I say. All things are like dreams, like illusions or magical effects; therefore errant thoughts are basically silent, while material objects are basically empty. The emptiness of all things is not obscure to open awareness; so this mind with open awareness of silence and emptiness is your original countenance. It is also the seal of Dharma esoterically transmitted by the Buddhas of past, present, and future, the Zen Masters of successive generations, and all genuine teachers in the world.

33   If you realize this mind, this is really what is called ascending directly to the stage of Buddhahood without climbing up the steps. Your every footstep transcends the triple world; returning home, you put an end to doubt all at once. Then you are a teacher of the human and the celestial. With compassion and wisdom supporting each other, you fulfill both self-help and help for others. Worthy of human and celestial support, you are able to use ten thousand ounces of gold in a day. If you are like this, a great person in the real sense, your task in life is done.

34   Question: In terms of my present state, what is the mind of open awareness of silence and emptiness?

35   Answer: What enables you to ask me this question is your mind of open awareness of emptiness and silence; why do you still seek outside instead of looking within? I will now point directly to the original mind in you, to enable you to awaken; you should clear your mind to listen to what I say.

36   Throughout the twenty-four hours of the day, you oper-

ate and act in all sorts of ways, seeing and hearing, laughing and talking, raging and rejoicing, affirming and denying: now tell me, ultimately who is it that can operate and act in this way?

If you say it is the physical body operating, then why is 37 it that when people's lives have just ended and their bodies have not yet decomposed at all, their eyes cannot see, their ears cannot hear, their noses cannot smell, their tongues cannot talk, their bodies do not move, their hands do not grip, their feet do not step? So we know that what can see, hear, and act must be your basic mind, not your physical body.

Indeed, the gross elements of this physical body are 38 inherently empty, like images in a mirror, like the moon reflected in water; how can they be capable of perfectly clear and constant awareness, thoroughly lucid, sensitive and effective, with countless subtle functions? Thus it is said, "Spiritual powers and subtle functions—drawing water and hauling wood."

But there are many ways of access to the principle. I will 39 point out one entryway, by which you can return to the source. Do you hear the cawing of the crows and the chattering of the jays?

[Student's response:] I hear them. 40

Now turn around and listen to your hearing essence; are 41 there still so many sounds in it?

[Student's response:] When I get here, all sounds and all 42 discriminations are ungraspable.

Marvelous, marvelous! This is the Sound Seer's gateway 43 into the principle. Now let me ask you further: You say that when you get here all sounds and all discriminations are totally ungraspable. Since they cannot be grasped, does that not mean that there is empty space at such a time?

14   [Student's response:] Originally not empty, it is clearly not obscure.

15   What is the substance that is not empty?

16   [Student's response:] It has no form; there is no way to express it in words.

17   This is the life of the Buddhas and Zen masters; do not doubt anymore. Since it has no form, could it have size? Since it has no size, could it have bounds? Because it has no bounds, it has no inside or outside. Having no inside or outside, it has no far or near. With no far or near, there is no there or here. Since there is no there or here, there is no going or coming. Because there is no going or coming, there is no birth or death. Having no birth or death, it has no past or present. With no past or present, there is no delusion or enlightenment. There being no delusion or enlightenment, there is no ordinary or holy. Since there is nothing ordinary or holy, there is no pollution or purity. Because there is no pollution or purity, there is no judgment of right and wrong. With no judgment of right and wrong, all terms and statements are ungraspable. Once there are no such subjective states and false ideas, then all sorts of appearances and all sorts of labels are ungraspable. Is this not original empty silence, original nothingness?

18   However, in the state where all things are empty, open awareness is not obscured; this is not the same as being insentient. The release of your own spirit is the pure substance of your mind, with open awareness of empty silence. And this pure, open, tranquil mind is the supremely pure luminous mind of the Buddhas of past, present, and

future. It is also the essence of awareness that is the root source of all living beings.

Those who realize this and keep to it sit in one suchness 49 and are immutably liberated. Those who stray from this and turn away from it traverse the six courses and go round and round for eternity. Therefore it is said that straying from the One Mind to traverse the six courses is "departure," or "disturbance," while awakening to the realm of reality and returning to the One Mind is "arrival," or "tranquillity."

Even though there is a difference between whether one 50 strays from it or realizes it, nevertheless the basic source is one. That is why it is said that the Dharma refers to the minds of the living beings. This open, silent mind is not more in sages or less in ordinary people. Thus it is said that in sages it is knowledge that is nevertheless not flashy, and while it is hidden in the ordinary mind, yet it is not dimmed.

Since it is not more in sages or less in ordinary people, 51 how could the Buddhas and Zen masters be different from other people? What makes them different from other people is simply that they are able to guard their own minds and thoughts. If you can trust completely, your feelings of doubt will stop all at once, allowing a healthy will to emerge, so that you can discover real true vision and understanding, personally tasting its flavor, so that you naturally arrive at the stage of spontaneous acknowledgment.

This is the understanding of someone who is going to 52 cultivate the mind; there are no more stages or steps, so it is called sudden. It is like the saying that real faith is

attained only when there is conformity to perfect Buddhahood in the basis of your faith.

53   Question: If there are no more stages after having realized this principle, why the need for subsequent practice,
gradual cultivation, and gradual perfection?

54   Answer: I have already explained the meaning of gradual
practice after enlightenment, but seeing that your doubts
have not yet been resolved, I will explain it again. You
should purify your mind so as to listen truly and hear accurately.

55   Ordinary people have been revolving in circles since
time immemorial, being born and dying in five courses of
existence. Because of clinging fixedly to self-images, false
ideas, and misperceptions, the habits of illusion eventually
become second nature to them. Even if they suddenly
awaken in this life and realize that their essential nature is
fundamentally empty and silent, no different from the
Buddhas, nevertheless past habits are difficult to remove all
at once.

56   Therefore they rage and rejoice as they encounter irritating and pleasing situations; judgments of right and wrong
arise and pass away in profusion, and afflictions caused by
outside influences are no different from before. If they do
not make use of the power within transcendent insight,
how can they quell ignorance and reach the state of great
rest and tranquillity? As it is said, "When suddenly awakened, although you are the same as Buddha, the energy of
many lifetimes of habits is deep seated. Though the wind
stops, the waves still billow; though noumenon is manifest,
thoughts still invade."

57   Master Gao also said, "Time and again those who have

sharp faculties awaken without much effort, then they become complacent and neglect further cultivation. Eventually they drift back into their former confusion, unable to escape revolving in circular routines." So how can we neglect subsequent cultivation because of a single awakening?

Therefore, after awakening it is necessary to always   58
observe and examine yourself. When errant thoughts suddenly arise, do not go along with them at all; reduce them, reduce them, until you reach the point of noncontrivance, which alone is the ultimate end. This is the ox-herding practice carried out by all illuminates after their enlightenment. Even though there is subsequent cultivation, they have already realized sudden enlightenment.

Errant thoughts are fundamentally empty; the essence of   59
mind is fundamentally pure. To stop evil over and over without any stopping, and cultivate goodness over and over without any cultivating, is true stopping and cultivation. Therefore it is said that even as you fully cultivate myriad practices, only no thought is to be considered a basis.

In making a general distinction between the meanings of   60
attaining enlightenment first and then cultivating it afterward, Guifeng said, "You suddenly realize this essence is originally free from afflictions; the essence of uncontaminated knowledge is inherently complete, no different from Buddha. To cultivate practice based on this is called the Zen of the highest vehicle, and it is also called the pure Zen of those who realize suchness. If you can cultivate its practice moment to moment, in a gradual manner you will naturally attain hundreds and thousands of spiritual states. This is the Zen that has been transmitted in the school of

Bodhidharma." Thus sudden enlightenment and gradual cultivation are like the two wheels of a chariot; it will not work if one is missing.

61   Some people, not knowing the essential emptiness of good and evil, think practical cultivation of mind means to sit rigidly immobile, subduing body and mind, like a rock placed on top of grass. This is ludicrous. That is why it is said that followers cut off confusion in every state of mind, yet the mind that does the cutting off is a brigand.

62   Just clearly observe that killing, stealing, rapine, and falsehood arise from nature, arising without any arising, and they will immediately be annulled. Then what further need to stop them is there? That is why it is said that we should not fear the arising of thoughts, just fear being slow to notice. It is also said, "When thoughts arise, immediately notice them; once you become aware of them, they are no longer there."

63   Thus in the experience of enlightened people, even if there are afflictions associated with the external world, all of them produce the most subtle and refined flavor. Just be aware that confusion has no basis, that the illusory triple world is like smoke swirling in the wind, that the phantasmagoric six sense fields are like hot water melting ice.

64   If you can practice this moment to moment, not neglecting to be attentive, seeing to it that concentration and insight are equally sustained, then love and hate will naturally lighten and thin out, while compassion and wisdom will naturally increase in clarity; sinful deeds will naturally end, while meritorious actions will naturally progress.

65   When afflictions are ended, then birth and death stop. If subtle flowings are permanently ended, the great knowledge

of complete awareness alone remains, radiantly clear. Then you manifest millions of emanation bodies in the lands of the ten directions, responding to potential as sensed, like the moon appearing in the highest skies with its reflection distributed throughout myriad waters, functioning adaptively to liberate boundless beings with affinity, joyful and happy, without sorrow. This is called great enlightenment, honored by the world.

Question: The meaning of equally sustaining concentra- 66
tion and insight in the process of gradual cultivation is not really clear yet. Please explain further, with detailed instruction to break through confusion and lead us into the door of liberation.

Answer: If we set up principles for entry into inner truth, 67
there may be a thousand methods, but all of them are within the categories of concentration and insight. To sum up their essentials, they are just the substance and function of our own essential nature. These are the aforementioned empty silence and open awareness.

Concentration is the substance, insight is the function. 68
Being function identical to substance, insight is not apart from concentration; being substance identical to function, concentration is not apart from insight. As Caoqi said, "The ground of mind has no confusion, it is inherently stable; the mind of ground has no folly, it is inherently wise."

If you awaken like this, then the detachment and illumi- 69
nation of silence and awareness are not two. This is the sudden way, in which one cultivates both concentration and insight together as a pair.

If we speak of first using profound silence to quell 70
conditioned thinking and then using alert awareness to

41

quell oblivion, these initial and subsequent remedies balanced and harmonized to lead into tranquillity, this is considered the gradual way. This is the practice of those of inferior potentials; although they say alertness and silence are equally maintained, nevertheless they hold to tranquillity as a practice. How could they be considered people who have completed their work, who are never apart from fundamental silence and fundamental awareness, naturally practicing simultaneous cultivation of both? As Caoqi said, "Spontaneous enlightenment and cultivation of practice are not in quietude; if you are a quietist from beginning to end, you are confused."

71   Thus for adepts the principle of equally maintaining concentration and insight is not a matter of effort; it is spontaneous and effortless, with no more particular time frame. When seeing and hearing, they are just so; when dressing and eating, they are just so; when defecating and urinating, they are just so; when conversing with people, they are just so; whatever they are doing, walking, standing, sitting, reclining, speaking, silent, rejoicing, raging, at all times and in everything they are thus, like empty boats riding the waves, going along with the high and the low, like a river winding through the mountains, curving at curves and straight at straits, without minding any state of mind, buoyantly going along with nature today, going along with nature buoyantly tomorrow, adapting to all circumstances without inhibition or impediment, neither stopping nor fostering good or evil, simple and straightforward, without artificiality, perception normal.

72   Then there is not a single atom to make into an object; so why bother to work to clear anything away? Without a

42

single thought producing feelings, there is no need for the power to forget mental objects.

However, those who obstructions are thick, whose habits   73
are heavy, whose vision is lowly, and whose mind is unstable, those in whom ignorance is powerful and insight is weak, those who cannot avoid being altered by distur-bance and quietude in dealing with good and bad situations, whose minds are not peaceful, cannot do without the work of forgetting mental objects and clearing up the mind.

As it is said, when the six sense faculties are in a   74
controlled state so that the mind does not go along with objects, that is called concentration; when mind and envi-ronment are both empty and radiant awareness is free from confusion, that is called insight.

Although this is a formal approach, a gradual approach   75
to concentration and insight, something practiced by those of inferior potential, nevertheless it cannot be omitted in the context of remedial teachings and practices.

If there is a lot of excitement, you first use concentration   76
to conform to noumenon and rein in the scattered mind; by not going along with mental objects, you merge with original silence.

If there is a lot of oblivion, then next you use insight to   77
analyze things and contemplate emptiness; when conscious-ness is free from confusion, you merge with original awareness.

You quell random imagination by concentration, and   78
quell insensibility by insight. When disturbance and qui-etude are both forgotten, curative work is done. Then when dealing with things, each passing thought returns to the

source; encountering situations, each state of mind merges with the Way.

79   Only when you spontaneously practice both together are you considered free. If you are like this, you can truly be called one who maintains concentration and insight equally, and clearly sees Buddha-nature.

80   Question: According to the distinctions you have made, there are two meanings to equal maintenance of concentration and insight in the process of cultivation in the aftermath of enlightenment. One of them involves spontaneous concentration and insight, the other involves formal concentration and insight.

81   In reference to spontaneous concentration and insight, you have said that naturally occurring silent awareness is originally uncontrived and there is not a single atom to make into an object; so why bother to work to clear anything away? Without a single thought producing feelings, there is no need for the power to forget mental objects.

82   In describing formal concentration and insight, you have spoken of conforming to principle, concentrating the scattered mind, analyzing phenomena, contemplating emptiness, balancing and tuning the mind to eliminate oblivion and distraction, so as to lead into noncontrivance. In making the distinction, you say that this is the gradual approach, which is practiced by those of lesser potential.

83   I am not without doubt about the two approaches to concentration and insight. If you say that they are to be practiced by one and the same individual, does that mean that one first relies on the dual practice of spontaneous concentration and insight, then after that also applies the

curative work of formal concentration and insight? Or is it that one first relies on the formal approach to balance and tune out oblivion and distraction, and then after that enters thereby into spontaneous concentration and insight?

If we first rely on spontaneous concentration and insight, 84 they are natural silence and awareness, so there is no more curative work; why should we then also take up formal concentration and insight? This would be like losing the quality of white jade by carving a design on it.

If we first use formal concentration and insight until their 85 curative effect is achieved, and then proceed to spontaneous concentration and insight, then this is the same as the gradual cultivation practiced prior to enlightenment in the gradual approach by those of inferior faculties; how could it be called a sudden approach, which is to first awaken and then cultivate practice afterward, using effortless effort?

If they are simultaneous, with neither preceding the 86 other, yet the two kinds of concentration and insight, sudden and gradual, are different, how could they be practiced at once? Thus the individual taking the sudden approach relies on the spontaneous way, effortlessly going along with the flow; those of lesser potential taking the gradual approach follow the formal way, exerting effort at curative measures. The potentialities for which the two approaches are suited, the sudden and the gradual, are not the same; it is clear that one is superior to the other. How can initial enlightenment and subsequent practice both be analyzed into two types? Please give us a comprehensive explanation to enable us to put an end to doubt.

Answer: The analysis is perfectly clear; you are produc- 87 ing your own subjective doubts. Pursuing the words and creating interpretations, you create more and more doubt and confusion. When you get the meaning, you forget the words and do not bother to press the issue. But let me address the individually distinct modes of practice within the two approaches.

88   To practice spontaneous concentration and insight is the sudden approach, using effortless effort, both operative yet both tranquil, spontaneously cultivating intrinsic essence, naturally fulfilling the Way of Buddhas. To practice formal concentration and insight is the gradual approach taken before enlightenment by those of lesser potential, using curative work, striving to direct each thought toward cutting off confusion and grasping quietude.

89   The practices of these two approaches, sudden and gradual, are individually different and not to be mixed up. When we also discuss formal curative practices within the process of gradual cultivation after enlightenment, this does not include everything that is practiced by those whose potentialities require a gradual approach. It is just a matter of temporarily taking expedient ways.

90   And why is this? Because among those who are suited to the sudden approach, there are also those whose potentials are superior and those whose potentials are inferior. Thus their practice cannot be judged by the same standard.

91   As for those whose afflictions are slight, who are light and easy in body and mind, who are detached from good in the midst of good and detached from evil in the midst of evil, who are unmoved by the eight winds and calmly accept the three kinds of sensations, they rely on spontaneous concentration and insight, which they cultivate simultaneously without effort, naturally real and uncontrived, al-

ways in meditation whether active or still, and fulfill the design of nature. Why should they pursue formal practices for curative purposes? When there is no illness, one does not seek medicine.

As for those who, in spite of having first realized sudden ₉₂ awakening, have deep afflictions and rigid mental habits, who give rise to feelings toward objects thought after thought, who create confrontations with situations in every state of mind, who are thereby befuddled and confused, killing and obscuring the normalcy of their silent awareness, it is appropriate for them to make provisional use of formal concentration and insight, not neglecting curative measures, balancing and tuning their minds to eliminate oblivion and distraction, thereby to enter into noncontrivance. Even though they make temporary use of curative practices to tune out their habit energies, because they have already attained sudden realization of the fundamental purity of the essence of mind and the fundamental emptiness of afflictions, therefore they do not fall into the affected practice of those with inferior potentialities who take the gradual approach.

Why is this? When practice is cultivated before awaken- ₉₃ ing, then even if you work unremittingly, cultivating practice every moment, you will conceive of one doubt after another as you go along and will be as yet unable to attain nonobstruction. It will be like having something stuck in your chest; signs of uneasiness will always be present. If curative practices are developed to maturity over a long period of time, then body and mind seem lightened and eased of acquired pollution, but even though you are light and easy, as long as you have not cut through the root of doubt, curative practices are like stones placed on grass; you have still not attained freedom in the realm of birth and death. That is why it is said that when practice is before enlightenment, it is not real practice.

94   As for people who have realized enlightenment, even though they may have expedient techniques as curative measures, they never have a thought of doubt and do not fall into affected habits; over a period of time they naturally attain perfect accord. The naturally real subtle essence is spontaneously silently aware, focusing on all objects with each passing thought while annihilating all afflictions in each passing state of mind. This is not distinct from fulfilling supreme enlightenment by equal maintenance of spontaneous concentration and insight. So even though formal concentration and insight are practiced by those with potential suited for the gradual approach, for people who have realized enlightenment they can be said to transmute iron into gold.

95   If you know this, then how can you entertain doubts based on dualistic views, just because the two approaches to concentration and insight have an order of precedence? I hope that people who study the Way will examine and savor these words and stop entertaining doubts and inhibiting themselves. If they have a strong will to seek supreme enlightenment, what other recourse do they have if they reject this?

96   Do not cling to the letter, just comprehend the meaning, referring each point to your own self, so as to merge with the original source. Then the knowledge that has no teacher will spontaneously appear, the pattern of natural reality will be perfectly clear, unobscured, and you will attain the body

of wisdom, attaining enlightenment without depending on anyone else.

However, even though this sublime teaching is for every-   97
one, unless they have already planted seeds of wisdom and have the faculties and capacity for the Great Vehicle, they cannot conceive a thought of genuine faith. And not only will they not believe in it, from time to time there are even those who slander and revile it, calling uninterrupted hell upon themselves.

Even if you do not believe or accept the teaching, once   98
it passes by your ears it temporarily forms a connection The merit of this, the virtue of this, cannot be measured. As it says in *The Secret of Mind Alone*, "If you hear but do not believe, that still forms a cause of Buddhahood; if you study but do not attain, that still increases the blessings of humans and celestials, not losing the true foundation of Buddhahood. How much the more infinite are the merit and virtue of those who hear and believe, study and attain, preserve intact and do not forget? How can their merit and virtue be measured?"

When we think back to past routine actions, who knows   99
for how many thousands of aeons we have gone by way of darkness into uninterrupted hell, experiencing all sorts of misery of who knows how many kinds. So if we want to seek the Buddha Way, unless we meet good friends we will be forever sunk in darkness, unconsciously doing evil deeds.

Sometimes we may reflect on this and unconsciously   100
heave a sigh of lament. How can we relax and take it easy, when it means experiencing the same troubles all over again? And who knows who may ever again enable us to find this path of cultivating realization open and unob-

scured? This can be called a blind tortoise finding a piece of driftwood, a minute seed hitting a needle.

101   What is more felicitous than the Way? If we get bored and backslide now, or if we get lazy and are always looking back, the minute we lose our lives we will fall back into evil dispositions and suffer all sorts of pains; then even if we wish to hear a single line of Buddhist teaching, believe and understand it, accept and hold it, in order to escape from the agony, how could that be possible?

102   When you are on the brink of destruction, it is useless to have regrets. I pray that people who practice the Way will not become heedless and not cling to greed and sensuality but will strive as diligently as if they were saving their heads from burning, not forgetting to notice that impermanence is swift, the body is like the morning dew, life is like the setting sunlight. Although we are here today, tomorrow cannot be guaranteed. Keep this in mind! Keep this in mind!

103   Even if you temporarily rely on mundane created goodness, you can still escape from the miserable routines of the worst states of being and attain exceptional rewards in higher states of being, experiencing all sorts of bliss. How much the more of this most profound teaching of the supreme vehicle; the merit and virtue produced just by momentarily conceiving faith in it are such that no simile can convey the slightest amount thereof.

104   As scripture says, "If someone fills the worlds of a billion-world galaxy with precious substances and gives them as offerings to the living beings of those worlds, causing them all to be fulfilled, and also teaches all the living beings of those worlds to attain the four realizations, the merit of that would be measureless and boundless but would not be

equal to the merit and virtue attained by thinking about this Teaching correctly for even the time it takes to eat a meal."

So we know that this teaching of ours is most noble, 105 most valuable, beyond comparison to any merit or virtue. Therefore scripture says, "A moment of pure consciousness is the site of enlightenment; it is better than building countless jewel shrines. The jewel shrines will eventually crumble into dust, whereas an instant of pure consciousness attains true awakening."

I pray that people who practice the Way will study and 106 savor these words, keeping them earnestly in mind. If you do not liberate yourself in this lifetime, then in what lifetime will you liberate yourself? If you do not cultivate practice now, you will miss out for myriad aeons; but if you do cultivate practice now, even if it is difficult, it will gradually become easier, until the work progresses of itself.

How unfortunate it is that people today are starving, and 107 yet when they encounter a royal feast, they do not have the sense to partake of it. They are sick, and yet when they meet a master physician, they do not have the sense to take the medicine prescribed. "I cannot do anything for those who do not ask themselves what to do."

Furthermore, constructed worldly affairs have forms that 108 can be seen and effects that can be tested. When people attain one thing, it is regarded as wonderful. This mind-source of ours has no perceptible shape or visible form; there is no way to talk about it, no way to think about it. Therefore demons and outsiders have no opening to slander it, while the gods cannot adequately praise it. So how can ordinary people with shallow perception describe it?

What a pity! How can a frog in a well know how wide 109

the ocean is? How can a jackal roar the lion's roar? So we know that people in this age of derelict religion, who when they hear this teaching marvel at it, believe and understand it, accept and hold it, have already worked for many sages and planted roots of goodness over countless aeons; they are those of highest potential, who have formed a profound affinity with the true basis of wisdom.

110   Therefore *The Diamond Scripture* says, "Those who are capable of engendering faith in these statements obviously have already planted roots of goodness in the company of infinite Buddhas." It also says, "This is expounded for those who set out on the Great Vehicle; it is expounded for those who set out on the Supreme Vehicle."

111   I pray that those who seek the Way will not be timid and weak but courageous and bold. The good causes of past aeons cannot yet be known; if you do not believe in excellence and are willing to be wretched, you will conceive ideas of difficulty and obstruction. If you do not cultivate this teaching now, even if you have good roots from former lifetimes, you are cutting them off now. Therefore you are in ever deeper difficulty, becoming even more alienated.

112   Now you have already arrived at the abode of the treasure; you should not go back empty-handed. Once you lose the human body, you cannot get it back even in ten thousand aeons; please make sure to be prudent with it! Could anyone with wisdom who knew where the treasure is paradoxically fail to seek it, instead spending an eternity lamenting poverty? If you want to get some treasure, let go of the skin bag.

ZEN MASTER EJŌ (1198-1282)

Absorption in the Treasury of Light

There is a chapter on light in the *Shōbōgenzō:* the reason for   *1*
writing this essay now in addition is just to bring out
the essential substance, the fact that the countenance of
Buddhism is absorption in the treasury of light.

This is the unobtrusive application of inconspicuous   *2*
practice, carried out by oneself and influencing others,
proper to people who have studied Zen for a long time and
have entered its inner sanctum.

The so-called treasury of light is the root source of all   *3*
Buddhas, the inherent being of all living creatures, the total
substance of all phenomena, the treasury of the great
light of spiritual powers of complete awareness. The three
bodies, four knowledges, and states of absorption numerous
as atoms in every aspect of reality, all appear from within
this.

The Flower Ornament Scripture says, "The great light of the   *4*
Lamplike Illuminate is supreme among auspicious signs:
that Buddha has entered this hall, so this place is most auspicious."

This great light of the Lamplike Illuminate pervades the   *5*
universe, without differentiating between the mundane and
the sacred: thus "that Buddha has entered this hall." The
reception of "thus once I heard" is itself "having entered
this hall."

6   Because "this place is therefore most auspicious," Shākya-muni Buddha received indications of future direction from the Lamplike Illuminate.

7   Because this one light extends throughout all time, if there were any attaining it, then it would have to be twofold.

8   *The Scripture on the Miraculous Empowerment of Vairochana Attaining Buddhahood* says, in the book on entering the state of mind of the method of mystical spells, "At that time the Blessed One said to the Thunderbolt Bearer, 'The will for enlightenment is the causal basis, great compassion is the root, skill in means is the ultimate.

9   " 'O Master of the Secret, what is enlightenment? It means knowing your own mind as it really is. This is unexcelled complete perfect enlightenment, in which there is nothing at all that can be attained. Why? Because the form of it is enlightenment; it has no knowledge and no understanding. Why? Because enlightenment has no form. Master of the Secret, the formlessness of all things is called the form of space.' "

10   The same scripture also says, "Master of the Secret, the practice of the Great Vehicle awakens the mind that transports you to the unconditioned, guided by selflessness. Why? Those who have cultivated this practice in the past have observed the basis of the clusters of mental and physical elements, and know they are like illusions, mirages, shadows, echoes, rings of fire, castles in the air. Master of the Secret, thus they relinquish the selfless, and the host of the mind autonomously awakens to the fundamental nonarousal of the essential mind. Why? Because what is before mind and what is after mind cannot be

apprehended. Thus knowing the nature of the essential mind, you transcend two aeons of yoga practice."

The fact that "before and after cannot be apprehended" 11 means that the light of great knowledge of Vairochana is like this because the essential mind is fundamentally unaroused.

The Flower Ornament Scripture also says, "The body of 12 Buddha radiates great light of infinite colors perfectly pure, like clouds covering all lands, everywhere extolling the virtues of Buddhahood. All who are illumined by the light rejoice; beings with pains have them all removed. Everyone is inspired with respect and develops a compassionate heart. This is the independent function of enlightenment."

The same scripture says, in "The Book on Awakening by 13 Light," "At that time the light passed a hundred thousand worlds and illumined a million worlds in the East. The same thing occurred in the south, west, north, four intermediate directions, the zenith, and the nadir. Everything in all of those worlds was clearly revealed. At that time, the enlightening being Mañjushrī in each place spoke up simultaneously before the Buddha in each place, uttering this verse:

'The Enlightened One is supremely independent,
transcending the world, relying on nothing,
imbued with all virtuous qualities,
liberated from all that exists,
undefiled, unattached,
free from imagination, without fixations.
His substance and essence cannot be measured;
those who see him all utter praise.

His light is everywhere, clear and pure;
the burdens of the senses are washed away.
Without moving, he detaches from the two extremes;
this is the knowledge of the Enlightened One.'"

So the knowledge of the enlightened is light, a concentration of the light of immutable knowledge beyond the two extremes of ordinary and holy, or absolute and conventional. It is the light of the nonconceptual knowledge of Mañjushrī, who represents great knowledge. This becomes manifest in the effortlessness of simply sitting.

14   For this reason Vairochana said to the Master of the Secret, "The practice of the Great Vehicle awakens the mind that transports you to the unconditioned, guided by selflessness." The Third Patriarch of Zen said, "Do not seek reality, just stop views." Obviously there is no ego in the treasury of light of the vehicle of the unconditioned, no opinionated interpretation. Ego and opinions are different names of spirit heads and ghost faces. This is just the light alone, not setting up any opinions or views, from the idea of self and ego to the ideas of Buddha and Dharma. Let us clearly hear transcendent wisdom being likened to an enormous mass of fire.

15   *The Lotus of Truth Scripture* says, "At that time the Buddha radiated a light from the white hair between his eyebrows, illuminating eighty thousand worlds in the East, pervading them all, to the lowest hells below as well as the highest heavens above." So this auspicious sign of light is the foremost, rarest of spiritual lights perfected by Buddhas.

16   The great being Mañjushrī said, in answer to the question of Maitreya, "This very auspicious sign of light appeared in

56

ancient times when the Buddha named Illuminate like a
Lamp made of the Sun and Moon expounded the Great
Vehicle, entering into absorption in the sphere of infinite
meaning. Now Shākyamuni Buddha must be going to expound the teaching of the Lotus Blossom of Sublime Truth,
which is for enlightening beings and kept in mind by
Buddhas."

So we should know that this light is the universal illumi-   17
nation of matchless, peerless great light completely filled
with infinite meaning. The great being Mañjushrī was at
that time called the enlightening being Sublime Light, and
was the eighth son of the Buddha called Illuminate like a
Lamp made of the Sun and Moon, who enabled him to
stabilize unsurpassed enlightenment. The last one to attain
Buddhahood was called Burning Lamp Buddha.

Hence we know that the sitting meditation of our school   18
is absorption in the treasury of light inherited directly from
Burning Lamp and Shākyamuni. What other doctrine might
there be? This is the light that is not two in ordinary people
and sages, that is one vehicle in past and present. It does
not let anything inside out and does not let anything
outside in: who would randomly backslide into cramped
boredom within the context of discriminatory social and
personal relationships? It cannot be grasped, cannot be
abandoned: why suffer because of emotional consciousness
grasping and rejecting, hating and loving?

Furthermore, in "The Book on Comfortable Behavior" [in   19
The Lotus Scripture] Mañjushrī is told, "Great enlightening
beings dwell in a state of forbearance, gentle, docile, and
not rough, their minds undisturbed. And they do not
ruminate over things, but see the real character of things,

and do not act indiscriminately." This is simply sitting: without acting indiscriminately, one thereby goes along in conformity with the great light.

A verse from the same book says,

"Delusion conceives of things as existent or nonexistent,
as being real or unreal, as born or unborn.
In an uncluttered place, concentrate your mind,
remain steady and unmoving, like a polar mountain.
Observe that all phenomena have no existence,
that they are like space, without solid stability,
neither being born nor emerging.
Unmoving, unflagging, abide in oneness:
this is called the place of nearness."

This is a direct indication, "only expounding the unexcelled Way, getting straight to the point, setting aside expedients."

20   In China, the great master Bodhidharma replied to the question of an emperor about the ultimate meaning of the holy truths, "Empty, nothing holy." This is the great mass of fire of the light of the Zen of the founding teachers: crystal clear on all sides, there is nothing in it at all. Outside of this light, there is no separate practice, no different principle, much less any knowledge or objects; how could there be any practice and cultivation, or deliberate effort to effect specific remedies?

21   The emperor said to Bodhidharma, "Who is it replying to me?" Bodhidharma said, "Don't know." This is simply the single light that is empty.

22   Later Zen master Xuedou wrote a eulogy of this anecdote:

" 'Empty, nothing holy'—
how to discern the point?
'Who is replying to me?'—
'Don't know,' he says."

If you can attain freedom and ease by absorption in this   23
koan, the entire body is luminous, the whole world is luminous.

The great master Yunmen, thirty-ninth generation from   24
the Buddha, said to a group in a lecture, "All people have a
light, but when they look at it they do not see it, so it is
obscure. What is everyone's light?" No one replied, so the
master himself said in their behalf, "The communal hall,
the Buddha shrine, the kitchen pantry, the mountain gate."

Now when the great master says that everyone has a   25
light, he does not say it is to appear later on, nor that it
existed in the past, nor that it becomes apparent to a view
from the side: he is stating that everyone has a light. This
is exactly what is meant in the overall sense by the light of
great wisdom: it should be heard and retained, enjoyed and
applied, in the skin, flesh, bones, and marrow.

The light is everyone: Shākyamuni and Maitreya are its   26
servants. What is not more in Buddhas or less in ordinary
beings is this spiritual light, so it is existent in all; it is the
whole earth as a single mass of fire.

The master said, "What is everyone's light?" At that time,   27
the assembly made no reply. Even if there had been a
hundred thousand apt statements, there still would have
been "no reply."

Yunmen answered himself in their behalf, "The commu-   28
nal hall, the Buddha shrine, the kitchen pantry, the mountain gate." This answering himself in their behalf is answer-

ing himself in everyone's behalf, answering himself in behalf of the light, answering himself in behalf of obscurity, answering himself in behalf of the assembly's lack of response: it is absorption in the treasury of light awakening and bringing forth radiant light.

29 This being so, it does not question whether you are ordinary people or Buddhas, it does not discriminate between sentient and inanimate beings: having always been shining everywhere, the light has no beginning, no location. That is why it is "obscure," it is "what," it is "traveling at night," it is "impossible to conceive of even in a billion billion million aeons."

30 Also, a monk asked Yunmen, "The light silently shines throughout countless worlds—" Before he had even finished posing his question, Yunmen quickly asked back, "Are these not the words of a famous poet?" The monk said, "They are." Yunmen said, "You are trapped in words."

31 Hail to the ancient Buddha Yunmen! His eyes were fast as comets, his mind swift as lightning! At this point the monk was speechless. Who would not be ashamed?

32 Zen master Xuefeng, instructing a group, said, "The Buddhas of all times turn the great wheel of the Teaching in flames of fire." Yunmen said, "The flames of fire expound the Teaching to the Buddhas of all times; the Buddhas of all times stand there and listen."

33 So the light of flames of fire is the site of enlightenment of the Buddhas of all times, it is the teacher of the Buddhas. For this reason, all of the Enlightened Ones are always expounding the Teaching in the midst of myriad forms even as they remain at their own site of enlightenment, which is the light of complete perfect tranquillity.

It is a matter of "valuing the ears without devaluing the eyes." This mass of flames of fire is not in front, not behind: it is just total manifestation.   34

To go on degrading yourself and limiting yourself in spite of that, producing individual subjective ideas that you are basically an ignorant ordinary being, a common person with no wisdom, is truly hellish behavior slandering the Wheel of True Teaching of the Enlightened.   35

The exposition of the Teaching by the flames of fire indicated by Xuefeng and expressed by Yunmen is a direct approach without expedients, just expounding the unexcelled Way, bringing out the totality of the teachings of the Buddha's whole lifetime.   36

When Xuefeng spoke as he did, this was already being burned up in the flames of fire. Do you want to escape? Reciting scriptures, performing prostrations, raising and lowering each foot—everything is the manifestation of the great function of light.   37

There are those who learn to wonder whose grace this depends on, uselessly toiling to quiet thoughts without knowing this hidden essence. There are also those who doubt and dismiss the possibility, making a living in a ghost cave. There are also those who go into the ocean to count the grains of sand. There are also those who are like mosquitoes breaking through a paper window. Leaving aside for the moment getting trapped in words, what would be right?   38

Although there is no more leisure time to wash a clod of earth in the mud, students of Zen should first know what is being said when they pose a question. Once we are talking about silent illumination pervading the universe, why   39 should these be the words of a famous poet? Why should they be the words of Buddha? Why should they be your words? After all, whose words would they be? "The communal hall, the Buddha shrine, the kitchen pantry, the mountain gate." Listen clearly, hear accurately.

40   Great Master Changsha said to a congregation, "The whole universe is the eye of a practitioner. The whole universe is the family talk of a practitioner. The whole universe is the total body of a practitioner. The whole universe is one's own light. In the whole universe there is no one who is not oneself."

41   So penetrating study of the Way of the enlightened requires diligence to learn and faith to attain. Unless you form an alliance with the family of Buddhas lifetime after lifetime, how can you grasp what you hear in a lecture like this? Make sure that you do not become further estranged and further remote from it.

42   Now the universe spoken of by Changsha is a single eye of the individual involved in Zen study. The entirety of space is the total body and mind. He does not grasp the holy or reject the ordinary; he does not say that confused people are not so while enlightened people are thus. What he does is point directly to your own light: don't defer this to Great Master Changsha.

43   This sermon is an all-inclusive talk within your nostrils, a freely adapted practical lesson within your eyes. There are those who specially bring up old model koans but never attain insight or knowledge all their lives. Every one of them is the child of a rich family but has no britches.

44   Also, hearing talk of light, ignorant people think of it as like the light of fireflies, like the light of lamps, like the

62

light of sun and moon or the luster of gold and jewels, groping for comparisons; trying to see shining radiance, they focus on the mind and figure inside the intellect, aiming for it as a realm of utter emptiness and total silence.

For this reason they stop movement and take refuge in 45 stillness, or they are unable to relinquish ideas of an actual entity or false ideas of the existence of something to obtain; or their thoughts of inconceivable mystic wonder go on and on unceasingly and they think too deeply only of its rarity. Such people, rice bags sleeping with their eyes open, are the only numerous ones.

If it were really an inconceivably mysterious matter of 46 such great import, why do you imagine you can reach it by thinking? This is the type of bedevilment characterized by understanding the quiet reflection of the conscious spirit as the sitting of Buddha. This is why the founder of Zen explained that there is nothing holy in openness, and it is not consciously known. To be given such an explanation is something that rarely happens.

Zen Master Changsha said, "The reason students of the 47 Way do not discern the real is simply that they continue to recognize the conscious spirit. It is the root of infinite aeons of birth and death, yet deluded people call it the original human being."

So to cultivate realization based on ideas about your own 48 mind and assumptions about what is to be attained is to cultivate the root of birth and death.

Now the reference made to the real and the original human being mean the openness of the light that is inherently there and perfectly complete. Outside of the openness of the light, what thing would you try to seek so greedily?

That is why there is no holiness, and it is not consciously known; it is only a holeless iron hammerhead, a great mass of fire.

49   Zhaozhou asked Nanquan, "What is the Way?"

Nanquan said, "The normal mind is the Way."

Zhaozhou said, "How should one approach it?"

Nanquan said, "If you try to head for it, you immediately turn away from it."

Zhaozhou said, "If one doesn't make any attempt, how can one know it is the Way?"

Nanquan said, "The Way is not in the domain of knowledge, yet not in the domain of unknowing. Knowledge is false consciousness, unknowing is indifference. If you really arrive at the effortless Way without a doubt, you are as empty and open as space: how can you insist on affirmation or denial?"

50   This is why the ancients, pitying those whose approach is mistaken because it is contrived based on cultivated power, painstakingly guided them by saying, "The Way cannot be attained by the conscious mind, nor can it be attained by mindlessness; it cannot be communicated by words, nor can it be reached by silence. As soon as you get involved in deliberation, you are ten million stages away."

51   People, can there be any idea of cultivating mind, or any transmundane phenomena or principles, outside of this conscious mind or mindlessness? Since it is said to be unattainable either by the conscious mind or by mindlessness, why not immediately give up false ideas of seeking mind or relinquishing mind?

52   Ordinary people who do not believe and are lazy, and are not even up to the level of this device, cling to illusory

definitions of self, rush around pompously in the dreamlike
evanescent world, unaware that they are possessed by
demons of worldly knowledge and intellectual acumen.
Their wits always at work, they imagine that the light of
which they have heard tell must be like a fiery comet
shooting from between the eyebrows of Buddha. Interpret-
ing meanings literally, they never even think of finding out
the real truth of the sages. Even if they appear in the world
as seasoned practitioners and adepts, they have no part
in higher study, so they cannot ascertain how the light
throughout the whole body, the light of the realm of
reality, covers the heavens and covers the earth. They are
charlatans clinging to forms, unworthy even of pity.

Shākyamuni Buddha said, "The light of lights is not blue,   53
yellow, red, white, or black. It is not matter, not mind. It
is not existent, not nonexistent. It is not a phenomenon
resulting from causes. It is the source of all Buddhas,
the basis of practicing the Way of enlightening beings,
fundamental for all Buddhists."

So the Realized One had emerged from absorption in   54
flowery light, empty in substance and essence, sat on the
regal diamond throne of a thousand lights, and expounded
the light of the discipline of unity.

It is clearly obvious that this light is not blue, yellow,   55
red, white, or black. It is just "the god of fire, crimson
through and through," it is "a clay ox running on the
bottom of the ocean," it is "an iron ox without skin or
bones." It being "neither matter nor mind," why stick a
sense of seeking in your chest and repeatedly pant over the
inner mind? Furthermore, it is not a causally effected

65

phenomenon: how could it be made by cultivating real- ization?

56   Truly this is the source of the Buddhas, fundamental for all Buddhists. Not only that, it is the light of the discipline of unity accepted and held by Vairochana Buddha since his first inspiration. Therefore it is an element of the ground of mind, detached from all labels and appearances; this is called the light of the discipline of the mind ground.

57   Shākyamuni Buddha said, "If people who expound the Teaching stay alone in deserted places, where there is utter silence and no sound of human voices, and read and recite this scripture, I will then manifest for them the body of pure clear light. If they forget a chapter or verse, I will expound it to them so that they may comprehend it flu- ently."

58   So when you read and recite this scripture, this is the self at that time therefore manifesting pure and clear light. The body and mind of the Buddhas are light. The land of all Burning Lamps is Eternally Silent Light. Pure Lands, bodies, and minds are all light; that is why we say there are eighty- four thousand lights, up to an infinite number of lights.

59   Zen master Puning Yong quoted the aforementioned story about the flames of fire expounding the Teaching, and recited this verse to his congregation:

> "One mass of fierce flames reddens the whole sky;
> The Buddhas of all times are right in the center.
> Having expounded the Teaching, now they are done;
> Above the eyebrows there rises a pure breeze."

60   In the process of finding out the inner sanctum of Buddhism, spontaneously penetrating vision of the flames of fire ex-

pounding the Teaching is thus. So one mass of fierce flames blazes through time: it comes from nowhere, has no form, has no differentiation, and so ultimately has no extinction. Because it is completely undifferentiated, it is the scenery of the original ground of all phenomena, all beings, and all Buddhas.

Why do students today not keep this in mind or believe 61 in it resolutely? Because they do not believe in it resolutely, they become lowly ignorant fools, not escaping vicious circles. They should ask themselves where the fault is, and see all the way through.

Those who are wedded to worldly conventions think that 62 illusory and ephemeral phenomena are really permanent, so they are completely preoccupied with gain and loss of mundane profit. Placing profoundly abiding trust in a life that is like a temporary lamp before the wind, which cannot be guaranteed even until tomorrow, where each outgoing breath does not ensure that another ingoing breath will follow, they rejoice and lament according to vicissitudes.

Even your physical elements will vanish in the funeral 63 pyre, like evaporating dew; although there is not so much as an atom of anything that you can cling to as your own, you spend your life taking it easy, as if you were master of yourself.

This does not depend on the teachings of the scriptures; 64 it is an evident truth, right before our eyes. Since it is a mass of roaring flames, therefore the Buddhas of all times are also herein, and so are all beings in all forms of life also herein. In this context, how are living beings and Buddhas different? Those who erroneously cling to the ego do not believe in the light, so they are *herein* arbitrarily making themselves bob and sink in birth and death. Those who see through to the light, in contrast, are *herein* realizing impartial unhindered universal knowledge.

65   Therefore Yongjia said, "Eternal calm is not apart from right where you are; if you seek, I know you cannot see. It cannot be grasped, cannot be rejected; within ungraspability it is attained just so. The ancient Nāgārjuna said in a eulogy of wisdom, "Transcendent wisdom is like a mass of fire; it is ungraspable on all four sides."

66   Although everyone hears and reads such great teachings, you study them as if they were only relevant to others. You do not free and ease your whole being, you do not penetrate the totality. Instead you say that you are lacking in capacity, or that you are beginners, or that you are latecomers, or that you are ordinary mortals who have not cut off a single delusion. You do not put down your former views or your self-image. Dwelling in the great treasury of light all day and all night, you turn yourself into a lowly hireling, roaming in misery, a longtime pauper.

67   This is your own conceit of inferiority, having forgotten the call of your noble origins. How sad it is to take up a nightsoil bucket and become a cesspool cleaner, thinking of the body of pure light as a defiled body full of misery. This is the saddest of sadnesses, which nothing can surpass.

68   The subjectivity of the self-image should be changed right away. Even if you talk about the major and minor teachings, the provisional and the true teachings, the phenomena and principles of the exoteric and esoteric teachings, and the subtle messages of the five houses and seven schools of Zen, as long as you retain your self-image, you wind up in birth and death.

This is why it is said that if you interpret reality by means   69
of the mind of birth and death, then reality will become
birth and death.

The idea of the self, the idea of a person, the idea of a   70
being, and the idea of a life are self-image. The idea of the
physical body, prejudiced views, false views, and fixated
views are self-image. Even the countless subtle veils of
ignorance between standard enlightenment and sublime
enlightenment are self-image. First it is called the idea
of self, or intellectual habit energy; even attachment to
principle, traces of enlightenment, and the view of equa-
nimity are all different names varying according to the
degree and seriousness of self-image.

If you wonder why this is, from the very first great evil,   71
perverted, and biased views even up to the last little bit of
subtle ignorance, when there is no self-image, what can be
called an idea of Buddha or an idea of Dharma? Who is
conscious of the veil?

For this reason Zen master Dōgen said, "First you should   72
be done with the ego. If you want to be done with the ego,
you should contemplate impermanence." This is direct
instruction from a heart of consummate magnanimity and
perfect sincerity.

"The Teaching on Pacifying the Mind," by the Great   73
Teacher of Shaolin says, "Why do people of the world fail
to attain enlightenment in spite of all their studies? They
do not attain enlightenment because they are self-conscious. Fully developed people do not worry in miserable
situations and do not rejoice in pleasant situations; this is
because they are not self-conscious."

A verse by an ancient illuminate says,   74

69

"Buddhas do not see themselves; wisdom is Buddha.
If you really have wisdom, there is no other Buddha.
The wise know the emptiness of the obstructions of sin;
Equanimous, they have no fear of life and death."

Not fearing life and death is because of not seeing oneself.
Not seeing oneself means not being self-conscious, not
having a self-image. The light of great wisdom is thus
impersonal, so the verse says that wisdom is Buddha.

75   In spite of this, you think that it is a matter of loving the
transitory body, which is like dew on the grass, like a
floating bubble; when it comes to the great light that is
your real body, you think it is an irrelevant discussion and
suppose that there must be something more grandiose.
Thus you waste your time talking about political conditions
and the status of pious donations, without any stable
practice reflecting consideration of how this idly passing
life will end up.

76   If you have any attainment of faith or practice within this
treasury of light, why would it be only your own personal
liberation? Requiting the four debts above, providing suste-
nance for those in the three realms of being below, mountains, rivers, and earth, your own body and others' bodies,
are all the light of suchness, illumining everywhere endlessly.

77   Great Master Caoshan said in a verse,

       "The essence of awareness, round and bright, the body
           without form:
       Do not force distance or closeness in knowledge and
           opinion.

Absorption in the Treasury of Light

When thoughts differ, they obscure the mystic being;
When mind diverges, it is not close to the Path.
When feelings distinguish myriad things, you sink into the
    objects before you;
When consciousness reflects many things, you lose the
    original reality.
If you understand completely what is in these lines,
Clearly you are trouble-free, as you were of yore."

This is a direct indication, a direct explanation, within the 78
treasury of light, which furthermore gives directions for
subtle cultivation of fundamental realization. It does not
matter whether you are a monk or a lay person, whether
you are a beginner or experienced; it makes no difference
whether you are sharp or dull, or how much learning or
knowledge you have. This just points directly at the formless body of the essence of awareness, round and bright,
which is utterly unique and unmatched.

The essence of awareness is the Buddha-nature. Round 79
brightness is a great light; it is the formless silent light of
your present illusory body. Therefore an ancient worthy
said, "The whole body has no form, the whole world does
not hide it."

If you still do not understand, then let me ask you this: 80
shattering your whole body and burning up your skin, flesh,
bones, and marrow, bring me one thing. At precisely such
a time, the living beings and Buddhas of past and present,
the ordinary mortals and sages of the three realms, myriad
forms and appearances, are all without exception the formless body.

Master Linji said, "The physical elements are not able to 81 expound the Teaching or listen to the truth. Your spleen, stomach, liver, and gallbladder are not able to expound the truth or listen to the truth. Space is not able to expound the truth or listen to the truth. So what can expound the truth and listen to the truth?" This independent spiritual light listening to the truth is the formless body. The ancient temporarily gave it a name for the sake of other people, calling it the "independent wayfarer listening to the truth."

82   Having spoken of the "round and bright formless body of the essence of awareness," everything has been explained in one line. Out of kindness the master goes on to speak of subtle cultivation, saying not to force distance or closeness in knowledge and opinion. Those who are close to false teachers learn only opinions and interpretations, claiming to have attained Zen beyond the Buddhas and Patriarchs by means of empowerment through study, claiming to be beyond the knowledge and perception of all others, claiming to be closer to the Zen potential than anyone else. This is a perverse mentality, possessed by the king of all demons. It is a heretical belief in having attained what one has not really attained.

83   Next, those who imagine identity and cling to appearances slack off and fail to progress simply say they are dullards; they are not studious, they are far from being learners. This is "idly producing opinions."

84   The arising of these two kinds of view, hating and loving, judging right and wrong, turns into intellectual and emotional feelings and thoughts. Therefore Caoshan cuts in two with one sword stroke, saying, "When thoughts differ, they obscure the mystic being; when mind diverges, it is not close to the Path." Does this not mean that we

should abandon false teachers and approach good companions? Through the profession of false teachers, people learn opinions and interpretations, thinking of near and far; this is "idly producing opinions."

"This Path" and the "Mystic Being" are the Sun Face and 85 Moon Face of the light, essence of awareness. Nevertheless, from within this light a single unaware thought arises, and the errant mind increases false imaginings. These are floating clouds blocking the round and bright moon of the mind. This is why the verse says "it is not close to the Path."

"When feelings distinguish myriad things, you sink into 86 the objects before you." The Buddha already said, "Mind, Buddha, and living beings—these three have no distinction." He also said, "There is only one truth." Even though you hear and read such great teachings, for your own part you arbitrarily contrast others and self, and discriminate between the noble and the base, the ordinary and the holy. Because of the beauty or ugliness of sound and form, because of poverty and wealth, loss and gain, you are taken by the objects before you. This is brought about by your reliance on intellectual views, by pride and disbelief infecting practice and realization.

"When consciousness reflects many things, you lose the 87 original reality." Buddhism originally adapted to myriad different types of potential, resulting in teachings great and small, temporary and true, half and full, partial and complete, exoteric and esoteric, meditation and doctrine, the Path of Sages and the Pure Land Way. It is not that there are not many facets to Buddhism, but if you cling to them intellectually, after all you lose the original reality.

"If you understand completely what is in these lines, 88

clearly you are trouble-free, as you were of yore." The way you "were of yore" means that there is no fabricated effort to cultivate realization; it is the formless body, sitting utterly still, without doubt. If you keep any intellectual interpretation on your mind, you are not trouble-free, you are not "as you were of yore."

89   Shākyamuni Buddha said, "There is nothing I gained from Dīpankāra Buddha to realize supreme perfect enlightenment." This is an expression of a meeting with Dīpankāra Buddha; it is "one statement that transcends millions." The light of this "nothing gained" should be studied.

90   Nowadays, those who shave their heads and wear black as latter-day followers of Buddha spend the days and pass the months illumined by the light of Dīpankāra, "The Lamp," but they do not wonder what Dīpankāra Buddha, The Lamp Illuminate, really is. Therefore they are not real students; they just make use of the appearance of renunciants in order to grab donations. In reality, they are actually vagrants and roustabouts.

91   If you deny this, let me ask you, what are the marks and refinements of the Lamp Buddha? You cannot say anything, yet you cannot say nothing; speak quickly, speak quickly!

92   How sad that you only learn of the Lamp Buddha as an illuminate of the past and do not know that the Lamp Buddha shines throughout all time. How then could you believe that it is teaching and attaining nirvana in your nostrils, in your eyes?

93   Now there is a group of the lowest type of hearer, who repeatedly weary of life and death and hurriedly seek nirvana, arousing their determination on the basis of the idea of something really existing and something being

attained. Adding religious greed on top of selfish conceit, their seeking mind never rests until they die. Teachers without perception praise them as good people of faith, so they take pride in egotistical clinging and possessiveness as diligent spiritual practice, eventually turning into ghouls.

To begin with, the Buddhist study of perpetual energy 94 and the pure transmission of immutable radiant concentration is not like your erroneous concentration, which approaches cultivation and realization as two stages and seeks intellectual understanding.

Master Baizhang said, "The spiritual light shines alone, 95 utterly free of senses and objects; the essence manifests, real and eternal. It is not confined to writings. The nature of mind is undefiled, originally complete and perfect in itself. Just detach it from false objects and it awakens to suchness."

This spiritual light is unbroken from the infinite past 96 through the infinite future; this is called perpetual energy. Utterly free of senses and objects, the essence manifests, real and eternal; this is called permanent stability of radiance. Trusting in this spiritual light, abiding peacefully, imperturbable, is called the supreme concentration of simply sitting.

So there must be different levels of depth and shallow- 97 ness, of levity and gravity, even in saying there is something attained. If you just cling to the appearances of phenomena and cultivate formal practices, seeking Buddha externally, distinguishing the real and the false in terms of writings and words, you may practice giving while dwelling on appearances, misconstruing this to be accumulation of merit, or cause your body and mind pain for the sake of annihilating sin and producing virtue, simply taking pride in this as diligence. This is not called attaining something.

98   Even if you put aside pen and ink, abstain from social relations, sit alone in an empty valley, live off the fruits of the trees and clothe yourself with grasses, and sit all the time without lying down, in your mind you are trying to stop movement and return it to stillness, cut off illusion completely, dwell only on absolute truth, reject samsara and grasp nirvana, despising the one and loving the other; all of this is possessiveness.

99   For this reason, the great teacher Yongjia said, "If you abandon existence and cling to emptiness, your sickness is still there. This is like plunging into fire to avoid drowning. If you reject imagination to grasp truth, the grasping and rejecting mind produces clever falsehood. Students not understanding how to apply developmental practice actually wind up recognizing a thief as their own offspring. The loss of spiritual wealth and destruction of virtues inevitably derive from this mind, intellect, and consciousness." So students should plunge body and mind into the treasury of light, free and ease the whole body in the light of Buddha, sitting, reclining, and walking around therein.

100   This is why the Buddha said, "Offspring of Buddha abide in this stage, which is the experience of Buddhahood. They are always therein, walking around, sitting, lying down." These golden words should not be forgotten for even a moment by those who aspire to be offspring of Buddha. "This stage" is the treasury of light; it is the one sole vehicle to Buddhahood. Do not let a single thought turning away from enlightenment to merge with material objects trans-

form this experience of Buddhahood into the experience of
animality or ghosthood.

Now tell me about the marks and refinements, about the   101
site of the nirvana, of Dīpankāra Buddha, of Shākyamuni
Buddha, of the seven Buddhas and generations of Zen
Masters who perpetuated the flame of the lamp: do you
investigate and study them as remote in time and space, or
do you learn and think of them as permanently present and
eternal? Would you say they are in the jewel citadel of
silent light?

You understand that "the true reality of Buddha is like   102
space," but at such a level, if you do not pass through and
beyond the cave of learned judgments and comparisons,
how can you be called masters of the inheritance of the
light of Buddha? You are jackals howling, clinging to the
body of a lion.

If you cannot investigate truth through your own eyes,   103
even if you shave your head and dress in black, you are
pitiful living beings. Even if you can interpret a thousand
scriptures and ten thousand treatises, you are "counting the
treasures of another house," you are "seafarers who know
there's something valuable but do not know the price."

Tell me, right now as you defecate and urinate, dress and   104
eat, ultimately whose experience is it? And what, moreover,
of the colors of the waters, the scenery of the mountains,
the coming and going of heat and cold, the spring flowers,
the autumn moon, thousands of changes, myriad transformations—what brings all this about? Truly this is a "countenance most wondrous, light illumining the ten directions."
It is "samsara and nirvana are like last night's dream." It is
"being is nonbeing, nonbeing is being." If not thus, even if

77

you speak of "always being there on Spiritual Mountain," it is a false teaching, it is specious discourse; even if you hear of "eternally silent light that neither comes into being nor passes away," I would say it is only talk, with no real meaning.

105   In a classic statement of the discipline of unity, Shākya-muni Buddha said, "Those who entertain the idea of self and cling to appearances cannot believe in this teaching, while those who cultivate realization that annihilates life are not fertile ground. If you want to foster the sprouts of enlightenment, so that the light illumines the world, you should calmly examine the real characteristics of phenomena: they are not born and do not perish; they are not permanent and yet are not annihilated, they are not one and yet are not different; they do not come and do not go. Do not conceive discriminatory ideas, even between learning and the state beyond learning."

106   So this classic statement of light illumining the world should be heard all the way through your bones, all the way through your marrow It is the subtle body in which the great function of the Buddhas of all times becomes manifest. Taking it upon yourself to put it into practice, would not everyone be overjoyed?

107   However, as I see students today, being grounded on ignorance, they spend their lives polishing day and night, expecting to eventually see through to the light in this way. Then again, some try to see this radiant pure light by practicing meditation to get rid of random thoughts flying around, repeatedly trying to beat out the flaming fires, hoping to see the eternally silent light thereby. If you think the total nonarising of thought to be right, then are wood,

stones, and clods of earth right? All of you are the lowest kind of hearer, who drowns while trying to avoid being burned. How foolish! Clinging to the sitting of the two vehicles and the inclinations of ordinary people, you want to realize supreme universal enlightenment; there is nothing more stupid and perverse.

For this reason it is said, "Those on the two vehicles may 108 be diligent but lack the spirit of enlightenment; outsiders may be intellectually brilliant, but they lack wisdom. Ignorant and stupid, petty and fearful, they think there's something real in the empty fist."

To cultivate the mind or seek the mind in this manner is 109 to be obstructed by calculating and figuring, burying the inherently perfect light. Not only that, it repudiates the true teaching of the Buddha and makes for uninterrupted hell.

Furthermore, countless abbots of monasteries from the 110 sixth century even up until now have been mere ignoramuses, deficient in wisdom, taking in the unseeing masses of egotistical and possessive people. Can we not pity them? Can we not feel sorry for them? Even those who from time to time emerge from that nest see spirits and ghosts, their thieving mind not yet dead.

Some of them may wrongly give definitive approval to a 111 temporary surge of energy, or it may happen that through a temporary inspiration they sit for a long time without lying down, so that the mind and consciousness are thoroughly fatigued, everything becomes the same to them, activity and function stop for a while, and thoughts quiet down; then they misunderstand this state, which resembles the solitary radiance of ethereal spirituality, misconstruing it to be the state where inside and outside become one, the original ground of the fundamental state of the essential self.

112 Taking this interpretation to Zen teachers who have no true perception, they present the view. Since the teachers have no eyes to perceive people, therefore they go along with the words of those who come to them, giving them worthless approval, so that they call themselves graduate Zen monks. Countless followers of the Way with shallow consciousness and little learning fall into this poison. Truly, even as we say it is the age of dereliction of the teaching, is it not all pathetic?

113 I humbly say to people who are real seekers, who have the same aspiration, do not cling to one device or one state, do not rely on intellectual understanding or brilliance, do not carry around what you learn by sitting. Plunging body and mind into the great treasury of light without looking back, "sit grandly under the eaves" without seeking enlightenment, without trying to get rid of illusion, without aversion to the rising of thoughts, and yet without fondly continuing thoughts.

114 If you do not continue thoughts, thoughts cannot arise by themselves. Like an empty space, like a mass of fire, letting your breathing flow naturally out and in, sit decisively without getting involved in anything at all.

115 Even if eighty-four thousand random thoughts arise and disappear, as long as the individual does not get involved in them but lets go of them, then each thought will become the light of spiritual power of wisdom. And it is not only while sitting; every step is the walk of light. Not engaging in subjective thinking step after step, twenty-four hours a

day, you are like someone completely dead, utterly without self-image or subjective thoughts.

Nevertheless, outgoing breathing and incoming breath- 116
ing, the essence of hearing and the essence of feeling, without conscious knowledge or subjective discrimination, are silently shining light in which body and mind are one suchness. Therefore when called there is an immediate response. This is the light in which the ordinary and the sage, the deluded and the enlightened, are one suchness. Even in the midst of activity, it is not hindered by activity. The forests and flowers, the grasses and leaves, people and animals, great and small, long and short, square and round, all appear at once, without depending on the discrimina-tions of your thoughts and attention. This is manifest proof that the light is not obstructed by activity. It is empty luminosity spontaneously shining without exerting mental energy.

This light has never had any place of abode. Even when 117
buddhas appear in the world, it does not appear in the world. Even though they enter nirvana, it does not enter nirvana. When you are born, the light is not born. When you die, the light is not extinguished. It is not more in Buddhas and not less in ordinary beings. It is not lost in confusion, not awakened by enlightenment. It has no location, no appearance, no name. It is the totality of everything. It cannot be grasped, cannot be rejected, can-not be attained. While unattainable, it is in effect through-out the entire being. From the highest heaven above to the lowest hell below, it is thus completely clear, a wondrously inconceivable spiritual light.

If you believe and accept this mystic message, you do 118

not need to ask anyone else whether it is true or false; it will be like meeting your own father in the middle of town. Do not petition other teachers for a seal of approval, and do not be eager to be given a prediction and realize fruition. Unconcerned even with these things, why then concentrate on food, clothing, and shelter, or about animalistic activities based on sexual desire and emotional attachment?

119   This absorption in the treasury of light is from the very beginning the site at which all Buddhas realize the ocean of enlightenment. Therefore it is sitting as Buddha and acting as Buddha, carried on in its utter simplicity. Those who are already Buddhists should sit at rest only in the sitting of Buddha. Do not sit in the sitting of hells, the sitting of hungry ghosts, the sitting of beasts, the sitting of antigods, humans, or celestial beings; do not sit in the sitting of hearers or those awake to conditioning.

120   Simply sitting in this way, do not waste time. This is called the enlightenment site of the straightforward mind, absorption in the treasury of light of inconceivable liberation.

121   This essay should not be shown to anyone but people who are in the school and have entered the room. My only concern is that there should be no false and biased views, whether in one's own practice or in teaching others.

MAN-AN *(17th century)*

An Elementary Talk on Zen

Although the Way of Buddhahood is long and far, ulti- 1
mately there is not an inch of ground on earth. Although it
is cultivated, realized, and mastered over a period of three
incalculable aeons, the true mind is not remote. Although
there may be five hundred miles of dangers and difficult
road, the treasure is nearby. If people who study Zen to
learn the Way mistake a single step or stir a single thought,
they are ten trillion lands and a billion aeons away.

You should simply see your essential nature to attain 2
Buddhahood. The scriptural teachings expounded by the
Buddha over the course of his career are instructions for
seeing essential nature; when it comes to seeing essential
nature itself and awakening to the Way, that is communicated separately outside of doctrine and does not stand on
written symbols.

In this there are no distinctions between the sharp and 3
the dull, the rich and the poor, mendicants and laypeople,
Easterners or Westerners, ancients or moderns. It only
depends upon whether or not the will for enlightenment is
there and whether instruction and guidance are mistaken
or accurate.

Even if you get directions from a thousand Buddhas and 4
myriad Zen masters, if you yourself do not continue right
mindfulness with purity and singleness of faith, you can
never see essential nature and awaken to the Way. This is

why you realize your own essential nature by means of your own mind and understand your own life by means of your own insight. If right mindfulness is not continuous and concentration is not pure and singleminded, your efforts will be in vain.

5   This right mindfulness means not having any thoughts; concentration means not conceiving any mental images. Zen master Dōgen said, "Thinking of what does not think is the essential art of sitting meditation."

6   If you concentrate intensely twenty-four hours a day, the same in activity as in quiet, principle and fact as one, then inward and outward bedevilments lose their ways of getting at you and you get beyond all obstruction. Good and bad, right and wrong, pain and pleasure, advantage and adversity, are shed all at once, the root compulsion by beginningless ignorance is severed, and you see the original state as it was before space and time.

7   "Before space and time" does not mean something remote in space and time; don't think of it as something ancient. It is the immediate experience of seeing essential nature right now: it is the time when you let go of your self and give up compulsion.

8   It should be understood, furthermore, that invocation of Buddha-names and recitation of scriptures are also sharp swords for severing the root of compulsion. Don't think that by accumulating effort and building up merit you will be reborn after death to see Buddha; don't seek resulting rewards of blessings and graces. You should be unattached to the marvelous.

9   As the past, present, and future mind cannot be grasped, right mindfulness appears spontaneously. Whatever you are

doing, concentrate wholeheartedly on questioning the inner master that perceives, cognizes, and emotes.

If your effort is weak, real wondering will not occur and 10 false imagining will be hard to expel. If you want to achieve early fulfillment, brandish the precious sword given by the mind king and march right ahead: if you meet Buddhas, kill the Buddhas; if you meet Zen masters, kill Zen masters; if you meet your parents, kill your parents; if you meet the masses of living beings, kill the masses of living beings. Totally massacre everything animate and inanimate, all forms and appearances, mountains, rivers, and earth, all times and all places, good and bad, right and wrong, plus anything else that appears and disappears, coming and going through the doors of the six senses and the alleys of the seven consciousnesses. Having killed it all completely, when you turn a flip and appear in the realm of cosmic space, you can be called a real hero. When you get to this point, you will not doubt that Buddhas and sentient beings, enlightenment and affliction, samsara and nirvana, heaven and hell, are all illusions.

In Zen study, you should not slack off for an instant. 11 Alerting your vital spirit as you breathe out and in, watching your step as you walk forth and back, be as if you were galloping on a single horse into an opposing army of a million troops, armed with a single sword.

As long as our concentration is not purely singleminded 12 in both activity and stillness, it will be hard to attain even a little accord. Concentration of right mindfulness should be cultivated most especially in the midst of activity. You need not necessarily prefer stillness.

There is a tendency to think that Zen practice will be 13

quicker under conditions of stillness and quiet and that activity is distracting, but the power attained by cultivation in stillness is uncertain when you deal with active situations; it has a cowardly and weakly function. In that case, what do you call empowerment?

14 Concentration of right mindfulness is a state of absorption that is in oneself twenty-four hours a day, but one does not even know it consciously. Even though you work all day, you do not get tired out, and even if you sit alone or stand silently for a long time, you do not get bored. To search out enlightenment with principle and fact unified is called genuine study.

15 If you want to quickly attain mastery of all truths and be independent in all events, there is nothing better than concentration in activity. That is why it is said that students of mysticism working on the Way should sit in the midst of the material world.

16 The Third Patriarch of Zen said, "If you want to head for the Way of Unity, do not be averse to the objects of the six senses." This does not mean that you should indulge in the objects of the six senses; it means that you should keep right mindfulness continuous, neither grasping nor rejecting the objects of the six senses in the course of everyday life, like a duck going into the water without its feathers getting wet.

17 If, in contrast, you despise the objects of the six senses and try to avoid them, you fall into escapist tendencies and never fulfill the Way of Buddhahood. If you clearly see the essence, then the objects of the six senses are themselves meditation, sensual desires are themselves the Way of Unity, and all things are manifestations of Reality. Entering

into the great Zen stability undivided by movement and stillness, body and mind are both freed and eased.

As for people who set out to cultivate spiritual practice 18 with aversion to the objects and desires of the senses, even if their minds and thoughts are empty and still and their contemplative visualization is perfectly clear, still when they leave quietude and get into active situations, they are like fish out of water, like monkeys out of the trees.

Even people who go deep into mountain forests, cut off 19 relations with the world forever, and eat from the fruits of the trees as ascetics cannot easily attain pure singleness of concentration. Needless to say, it is even more difficult for those who are mendicants in name only, or shallow householders, who are so busy making a living.

In truth, unless you have definite certitude of overwhelm- 20 ing faith, or are filled with overwhelming doubt or wonder, or are inspired with overwhelming commitment, or are overtaken by overwhelming death, it is hard to attain concentration that is pure and undivided in principle and fact, in action and stillness.

If you are wholeheartedly careful of how you spend 21 your time, aware of the evanescence of life, concentrating singlemindedly on Zen work even in the midst of objects of desire, if you proceed right straight ahead, the iron walls will open up. You will experience the immense joy of walking over the Polar Mountain and become the Master within the objects of sense. You will be like a lotus bloom- ing in fire, becoming all the more colorful and more fragrant in contact with the energy of fire.

Do not say that it is harder for lay people living in the 22 world of senses and desires to sit and meditate, or that it is hard to concentrate with so many worldly duties, or that one with an official or professional career cannot practice Zen, or that the poor and the sickly do not have the power to work on the Way. These excuses are all due to impotence of faith and superficiality of the thought of enlightenment.

23   If you observe that the matter of life and death is serious, and that the world is really impermanent, the will for enlightenment will grow, the thieving heart of egoism, selfishness, pride, and covetousness will gradually die out, and you will come to work on the Way by sitting meditation in which principle and fact are one.

24   Suppose you were to lose your only child in a crowd or drop an invaluable gem: do you think you would let the child or the jewel go at that, just because of the bustle and the mob? Would you not look for them even if you had a lot of work to do or were poor or sickly? Even if you had to plunge into an immense crowd of people and had to continue searching into the night, you would not be easy in mind until you had found and retrieved your child or your jewel.

25   To have been born human and heard true teaching is a very rare opportunity; so to neglect meditation because of your career is to treat the life of wisdom of the body of truths of the Buddhas less seriously than worldly chattels. But if you search for wisdom singlemindedly like someone who has lost a child or dropped a gem, one day you will undoubtedly encounter it, whereupon you will light up with joy.

26   People in all walks of life have all sorts of things to attend to; how could they have the leisure to sit silently all day in quiet contemplation? Here there are Zen teachers who have

not managed to cultivate this sitting meditation concentration; they teach deliberate seclusion and quietude, avoiding population centers, stating that "intensive meditation concentration cannot be attained in the midst of professional work, business, and labor," thus causing students to apply their minds mistakenly.

People who listen to this kind of talk consequently think 27 of Zen as something that is hard to do and hard to practice, so they give up the inspiration to cultivate Zen, abandon the source and try to escape, time and again becoming like lowly migrant workers. This is truly lamentable. Even if they have a deep aspiration due to some cause in the past, they get to where they neglect their jobs and lose their social virtues for the sake of the Way.

As an ancient said, if people today were as eager for 28 enlightenment as they are to embrace their lovers, then no matter how busy their professional lives might be and no matter how luxurious their dwellings may be, they would not fail to attain continuous concentration leading to appearance of the Great Wonder.

Many people of both ancient and modern times have 29 awakened to the Way and seen essential nature in the midst of activity. All beings in all times and places are manifestations of one mind: when the mind is aroused, all sorts of things arise; when the mind is quiet, all things are quiet. "When the one mind is unborn, all things are blameless." For this reason, even if you stay in quiet and serene places deep in the mountains and sit silently in quiet contemplation, as long as the road of the mind-monkey's horse of conceptualization is not cut off, you will only be wasting time.

.

30   The Third Patriarch of Zen said, "If you try to stop movement and resort to stillness, that stopping will cause even more movement." If you try to seek true suchness by erasing random thoughts, you will belabor your vital spirit, diminish your mental energy, and get sick. Not only that, you will become oblivious or distracted and fall into a pit of bewilderment.

31   You should use the two methods of cessation and observation to perfect discipline, concentration, and insight. Cessation is Zen concentration, observation is insight. In cessation the mind, intellect, and consciousness are inactive, preventing all misconduct, cutting off the root of unconscious compulsion; there is no transgression of precepts, major or minor. In observation there is no attachment to appearances of conduct, all ideas of self and things are emptied, obstructions caused by beginningless habitual actions are annihilated, and the spiritual light of the essential self shines through everywhere, inside and outside.

32   There is no cessation without observation and no observation without cessation. Combining the two truths of emptiness and conditional existence, the ultimate truth of the Middle Way is established.

33   Models for practice of sitting meditation and ways of applying the mind in concentration have come down through tradition from the Buddhas and Zen masters. You should know too that there are also types of sitting meditation typically practiced by seekers of individual liberation, seekers of heavenly states, humanitarians, and assorted cultists. Those who aspire to unsurpassed enlightenment should practice the sitting meditation of Buddhas and Zen masters.

Buddhas and Zen masters conceive great compassion 34 from the outset, never forgetting the great mass of living beings. Sitting in the lotus posture, keeping the body upright, maintaining correct mindfulness, cessation and observation, and tuning the breathing are essential arts of sitting meditation.

In a clean and uncluttered room or under a tree or atop a 35 rock, spread a thick sitting mat. Then loosen your belt and sit. First bend the right leg and put the right foot on the left thigh. Then place the left foot on the right thigh. Now put the right hand on the left leg, palm up; place the left hand palm up on top of the right palm, and let the two thumbs brace each other.

Sit straight, neither leaning backward nor forward, align- 36 ing the ears with the shoulders and the nose with the navel. With the eyes open as normal, keep watch over the tip of your nose. Do not close your eyes, for that will beckon oblivion and drowsiness. Rest your mind in the palm of your left hand, and have your energy fill your lower abdomen, waist and pelvic region, and legs.

Expanding the ocean of energy in the umbilical sphere, 37 take one deep breath and expel it completely through the mouth. Then close the lips and let fresh air enter through the nose in continuous subtle respiration, neither hurried nor sluggish. Being aware of the exit and entry of the breath, think of what is not thinking. If you concentrate intently, basic energy will naturally fill you and solidify you. Your lower abdomen will become like a gourd or a ball.

The rule for pacing meditation is to walk slowly, calmly, 38 and carefully, half a step with each breath, following a straight course around a square perimeter. When you want to get up from stillness to pace around, massage and move your body, rising calmly and carefully. Walk slowly, along a straight path.

39   Move the right foot first, then the left. Each time you take a step, let it be half the length of your foot, and move each foot in the interval of one breath. Watch the ground about seven feet in front of you, and stand up straight as you walk. When you want to turn, turn to the right. Walking forward, walking back, if your concentration is pure and single, truth will become manifest and there will be no subjectivity in your standpoint.

40   As for the method of tuning the breathing, after having settled in your seat, nurture your mental energy in the ocean of energy and field of elixir, not letting it push upward from the umbilical sphere. Breathe through the nose, neither too rapidly nor too slowly, neither panting nor puffing.

41   When you breathe out, know you are breathing out; when you breathe in, know you are breathing in. Focus your consciousness on your breathing, not letting consciousness go up or down or out or in, not thinking discursively, not making intellectual or emotional interpretations, not trying to figure anything out, simply being aware of outgoing and incoming breathing, not missing a single breath.

42   When this concentration becomes continuous, the physical elements of the body become well tuned, the internal organs are purified, the upper parts are clear and cool, while the lower parts are warm. Body and mind will spontaneously produce great joyfulness.

43   When you maintain an open, silent, radiant awareness

whether you are active, stationary, sitting, or reclining, vehemently arouse the intensest determination. At this time, if you have the slightest conscious discrimination, any thought of peace, bliss, or seeing essence, you will never be able to get out of birth and death, even in a hundred aeons and a thousand lifetimes.

If you have faith profoundly settled and galvanize the 44 concentration to bring on the Great Death, suddenly you will find "the bottom fall out of the bucket" and "kick over the alchemical furnace," passing beyond myriad aeons in a single instant, crushing the universe underfoot with a step. What is there to doubt or wonder about the saying of the Indian Zen master Prajñātāra, "Breathing out, I do not get involved in objects; breathing in, I do not dwell on mental or material elements"?

As a beginning, when inexperienced, if your breathing 45 becomes congested, constricted, and irregular, then rock your body forward and backward and left and right to refresh your mind. Expel the turbid energy from below the navel, in one to three breaths, with the breath passing through the nose, making it go from rough to fine, then having it go out and in very subtly.

If you become drowsy or distracted, then count your 46 breaths from one to ten, stopping at ten and repeating again from one to ten. In this manner, counting up to ten over and over again, you should mentally watch your exhalations with accurate mindfulness. Techniques such as visualization of the dissolution of the material elements, visualization of bones and flesh returning to their origins, and other such traditional exercises are also effective.

The secret of inner gazing and nurturing life and the 47

Immortalists' wondrous art of refining elixir are also based on the methods of tuning the breathing taught in Buddhism. When you apply your mind to it wholeheartedly, sitting meditation is really a way to present and future peace and bliss.

48   In a textbook of Immortalism it says, "What is most essential to nurturing life is refining the body. The subtle aspect of refining the body is in congealing the spirit. When the spirit congeals, energy accumulates; when energy accumulates, the elixir develops. When the elixir develops, the body is stabilized; when the body is stable, the spirit is whole."

49   Obviously the Elixir of Immortality is not a material thing after all. The spot one and a half inches below the navel is called the ocean of energy; this is the place where the basic energy is stored and nurtured. Below that is called the field of elixir; this is the site where vitality and spirit are melded. When spiritual energy always fills here, you remain free from sickness, robustly healthy, and live for a long time without aging. For this reason, realized human beings do not belabor their vitality and do not cramp their spirit.

50   The art of nurturing life is like maintaining a nation. Spirit is like the ruler, vitality is like the administration, energy is like the people. To care for the people is the way to keep the nation at peace; to be sparing of your energy is the way to keep your body sound. When energy is used up, the body dies; when the people are displaced, a country perishes.

51   An enlightened leader focuses concern on those below; an ignorant ruler acts whimsically toward those below. When rulers act whimsically, then cabinet members flaunt

94

their authority, counting on the ruler's favor and indulgence, paying no attention to the desperate straits of the people below. Greedy ministers plunder rapaciously, callous officials steal by deceit, the faithful and moral go into hiding, and the common people are embittered.

When concern is focused on those below, then taxes and 52 levies are modest and honest, rewards and punishments are not arbitrary, laws and measures are just, plenty and parsimony correspond to the season, the soil is fertile, the country is strong, production is abundant, and crops are fruitful. There is no wasteland, and no starvation among the people.

The human body is the same way. When vitality and 53 energy always fill the elixir field, then internal troubles do not act up and external evils cannot invade. The six bandits flee, the four demons hide. The sinews and bones are firm, there is good circulation of the blood, the heart is peaceful, and the spirit is robust.

If you lose concentration of accurate mindfulness, having 54 it snatched away by a distracting object or lured away by random associations, then bedevilments arise in profusion and consequences of past actions collect on your mind and bother you. Immorality, indulgence, false opinions, and conceit increase, even to the point of destroying the seed of Buddhahood.

It is pitiful how human beings are all imbued with wisdom 55 and virtue, and fully endowed with the wish-fulfilling jewel, yet they degrade themselves and impoverish themselves. Many of them say they have minimal potential, or they are sickly, or they are obstructed by their past history, or they are entangled by circumstances, or there are no teachers, or the teaching is degenerate, or they have professional jobs, or they are householders.

56   People also say by way of excuse that they have parents and children, they have dependents, they have family business, they have social responsibilities, they are impure, they have troubles, there is tomorrow, there is next year, there is the next life. Creating their own laziness and boredom, lax and passive, they do not arouse the determination to practice Zen, they do not question and concentrate, they do not investigate Zen and study the Way.

57   Regarding the three poisons and five desires to be inherent nature, seeking repute and profit by flattery and deviousness as a daily occurrence, not only do they waste this irreplaceable life, they also add on to evil habits from beginningless past and suffer all sorts of problems and pains into the endless future.

58   This is most pitiful, most frightful. Having happened to be born human and had the fortune to encounter the teaching of enlightenment, they do not understand the fluctuations of their minds and do not know where their bodies will end up. Abandoning their innate wealth and nobility, burying their inherent light, they do not even know that Buddha-nature exists.

59   It is a pity that the true teaching has deteriorated and people's knowledge is inferior. People who attain the Way are few, and genuine teachers are rare. The inspirations of students today are incorrect from the start; in the course of their studies, many go on false paths.

60   Even people who are supposed to have superior faculties and great determination, to say nothing of those with mediocre or lesser potential, not infrequently take fame and

profit for their inspiration and make pride their willpower. Without distinguishing whether teachers and colleagues are right or wrong, they insist on seeking enlightenment and marvels. Without letting go of fixations on their own bodies and minds, they seek only prominence and fame.

Even though some such people may occasionally seem to   61
be exerting intense energy, when they deal with concrete events they backslide and slack off. Facing objective circumstances, they interrupt their concentration, so it does not continue and the Great Wonder does not appear.

What a waste! They wind up dying in a ghost cave in a   62
mountain of blackness, developing nihilistic views; or else they remain fixated in the radiant light of spiritual awareness, conceiving views of Buddha, Dharma, and eternity. Some recognize spiritual radiance, alert yet silent, and compare it to suchness, the essence of things.

Even if people like this meet teachers with clear eyes,   63
they do not relinquish their own opinions to learn the Way. Even if they study the koans of the ancestral teachers of Zen, they do not bring them to mind with focused concentration. Coming to impenetrable and inscrutable Zen devices, they interpret arbitrarily by rationalization and intellectual discrimination, calling that penetration through to freedom.

Even those who are supposedly Zen teachers have not   64
cut off their mental routines and have not arrived at the intent and expression of Zen. Making their living on hallucinations and altered states, they violate the rules of conduct without fear of the consequences. Neglecting the unified work on the Way that includes reading scriptures, performing prostrations before Buddhas, and simply sitting,

they reject the refinement and development process that includes sweeping, drawing water, gathering firewood, and preparing meals. The Zen monasteries are like general stores at the crossroads, dealing in poetry and song, prose and verse, calligraphy and painting, calculating, stamps, tea, incenses, medicine, divination, and all sorts of other arts. They engage in trade and commerce whenever the opportunity or demand arises. Can you call this means of dealing with the masses for the sake of the people? It can hardly be called the will for Zen study.

65 Even if you are intelligent, psychic, eloquent, and learned, have examined all principles, mastered all doctrines, and clarified all teachings, even if you can radiate spiritual light and transform the atmosphere, can tame ghosts and wild animals, and can die while sitting or standing, even if you are virtuous enough to be the teacher of kings and lords, and are even called an incarnate Buddha, unless you disregard wealth, sensuality, reputation, and profit, you can hardly be called someone with continuity of true mindfulness.

66 The sad fact is that both the clergy and the laity are superficial in their attention to the Way. Those who abandon name and profit are really rare. Therefore the teaching centers make talks on Zen and lectures on classics their style, consider large crowds and plenty of donations to be a flourishing condition, think learning and talent are wisdom, and call fame and power virtues.

67 On the borderline of life and death, on the very last day, of what use will any of this be? One day when you suffer illness, false thoughts will increase all the more, the fire in your heart will back up, and you will agonize in pain. After

your breath stops, as the great king of the netherworld glares at you with angry eyes and questions you with an iron rod in hand, it will surely be a terrible scene.

When we observe the world closely, we find that more 68 people are killed by false thoughts than by physical diseases. False thoughts are more to be feared even than poisonous vipers.

When you detach from false thoughts, illness is actually 69 a teacher. Since ancient times a great number of people have attained power and seen essential nature while struggling with the agonies of serious illness.

If you become very sick, do not fear death or look back 70 on life. Don the armor of patience, bundle the bow and arrows of faithfulness and justice, mount the horse of valiant power, grasp the whip of diligence, set up the standard of the Way of Unity, make selflessness and having few desires your troops, make continuous concentration of true mindfulness your general, fortify the castle of the mind king in the ocean of energy and field of elixir, store the provender of the elixir of five energies, set in motion the strategy of freedom from thought and imagining.

Do all this, and even if four hundred and four battle lines 71 of sickness arise all at once, backed up by eighty-four thousand troops of bewilderment, and attack through every facet of consciousness and every feeling and emotion, still you will not be dismayed. When they ultimately surrender to the kindness and compassion of the mind king, submit to the power of the general, are cowed by the bravery of the troops, put down their weapons and give up, then you will have no opponents in the ten directions, no misery in your whole body. With right and wrong one suchness, all within the four seas will sing of great peace, and you will attain comfort and happiness in this world and the next.

72   A Chinese Zen master of the past once suffered from dysentery. When he was on the brink of death, he fought with the pain and misery to sit in meditation. After a while his abdomen growled loudly and convulsed, whereupon the dysentery remitted and he attained a great awakening.

73   A certain monk of my acquaintance once suffered from influenza so severe that he couldn't eat for eight days, running a fever so high that his tongue turned black. He suffered continuously day and night. At this point he was scolded by his teacher. Regretting that he was still unenlightened, realizing he had been in error, he suddenly made a solemn vow. With do-or-die determination, he rolled up his sleeping mat and bravely sat on it to concentrate in Zen meditation. When he did this, the misery and the fever of the sickness suddenly dispersed. Clear and cool inside and out, body and mind in a state of sublime joy, he realized fundamental ungraspability.

74   I also had a similar experience. When I was twenty-eight years old there was some trouble stemming from an argument, and I was poisoned. My whole body burned with pain, and for a while my arms and legs and torso turned purplish black. It would be hard to express the intensity of my pain and suffering.

75   At that point I conceived profound repentance. Here I had first been inspired at the age of seventeen, had looked for true teachers and entered Zen communities, studied Zen and worked on the Way, even standing in water and sitting in the snow, not lying down to rest, never forgetting the quest day or night, for over ten years. Then I spent a

winter retreat at a certain monastery, where I received the guidance of a teacher and thought I had passed through life and death and shed my self. Now that I was being tortured by this poison, I realized how my mind was not free. So I put forth an enormous effort to sit up, fighting the intense pain.

At this point, the first watch of the night had not yet 76 been sounded. Tuning my breathing with true mindfulness, I went into the vision of the physical elements disintegrating. All of a sudden my breathing disappeared and real vision appeared. Essence and forms both forgotten, true mindfulness continued.

Then there came the sound of a bell, echoing in space. 77 As I observed my own body and the appearances of others, it was all like an unbroken expanse of empty space. Then I intimately understood the preaching of the original body.

When I stirred my body and stretched my limbs, they 78 felt most extraordinarily supple and purified. The pains I had been suffering hitherto were like last night's dream, and my color also returned to normal. Physically and mentally exhilarated, I calmly rose from my seat and went outside. Looking to the east, I saw that it was already dawn.

After a little while, vomiting and diarrhea occurred all at 79 once. It was as if my guts had been used up, and I was only flesh and bones. Meeting death while alive, finding life in death, it was as if the poison had changed into a medicinal elixir. For the first time, I detached from the dualistic views of hatred and love and attained realization of the equality of enemy and friend.

There were also similar cases in ancient times, such as 80 the bodhisattva named Courageous Giving, who violated a precept, made a great vow in the midst of his consequent torment, and suddenly realized acceptance of beginninglessness. There have been those who were attacked by thousands of mosquitoes and attained enlightenment while battling with the sickening itch. There were also those who attained awakening while battling with the agony of being dismembered or having their skin and flesh burned and pierced.

81 Great Master Yunmen attained a major awakening on having his leg broken. Ninagawa Shinuemon realized awakening during an argument. The Shōgun Takauji attained peace of mind on the battlefront.

82 In this context, to "fight" means not to fear and not to get involved but just to establish concentration of true mindfulness. If you plunge right ahead, both the pain and errant thoughts will turn into a mass of spirit and become unified work on the Way.

83 If you lose concentration of right mindfulness, not only will you be physically and mentally tormented by false thoughts and perverse moods in this life, you will also continue eternal birth and death, suffering great pain. This has happened to countless people past and present, both clergy and lay folk.

84 Now then, if rulers lack concentration of true mindfulness, they cannot bring peace and security to the populace. If administrators lack concentration of true mindfulness, they cannot fulfill loyalty and justice. If ordinary people lack concentration of true mindfulness, they cannot fulfill their social obligations.

85 For this reason I keep repeating that you should make your attitude of faith certain and stable, turn everything

102

you do into a single koan, and continue concentration of right mindfulness without interruption.

Intensive Zen requires strength of spirit and intensity of concentration. Do not degrade yourself, do not let yourself be weakly, and do not debase yourself. The Buddhas and the Zen Masters were thus, and we are also thus. Who were the ancient kings, and who are we? Sages have horizontal eyes and vertical noses; we too have horizontal eyes and vertical noses. Breathing out and in, we do not borrow the nostrils of anyone else; stepping forward, stepping back, we do not use another's legs. Always keeping up this determination to transcend the Buddhas and Masters, searching into the root core of one's own mind, is called a robust will.

Here it is not a question of whether you are a mendicant or a layperson. It does not matter whether you are a man or a woman. It makes no difference whether you are keen or dull, more or less intelligent. It does not matter whether you have a lot of work to do or are at leisure. Those who make the great promise and undertake the great commitment, who are full of great faith and arouse the Great Wonder, do not fail to perceive essential nature, awaken to the Way, and attain the skin and flesh of the Buddhas and Zen Masters.

There have been many women with willpower surpassing that of great men, women who cultivated Zen practice and passed through the barriers of potential set up by the Buddhas and Zen Masters. Hundreds, even thousands, of enlightened rulers, wise ministers, laymen, and laywomen in India, China, and Japan have seen essential nature and realized truth.

89   If you do not liberate yourself in this lifetime, what lifetime will you wait for? Once this day has passed, that much of your life is gone too. With each passing thought, observe the impermanence of the appearances of the world and give up thinking there will be a tomorrow. With each step tread the Great Way of the mind source, and do not turn to another road.

89   You should let go your hand- and footholds, as if plunging off a precipitous cliff. When body and mind have died away at once, it is like standing right in the middle of cosmic space, like sitting in the center of a crystal vase. All of a sudden there will emerge the great state that is not ordinary, not holy, not Buddha, not mind, not a thing; you will attain penetrating realization that mind, Buddha, and living beings are one. This is the reality-body of all Buddhas, the inherent essence of all people. By realizing this, one becomes a Buddha or a Zen master; by missing this, one becomes an ordinary mortal.

90   Although people's faculties may be keen or dull, and practice and realization may be gradual or sudden, the secret I have been revealing here is the teaching of attaining Buddhahood by sudden enlightenment. It is a standard rule in which higher, middling, and lesser faculties are one whole. It is far from the gradual practice and learning of the two vehicles of individual liberation.

91   To think Buddha-nature is the state where mind is empty and objects are silent, where there is radiant awareness without arousing a single thought, is to consider the conscious spirit to be the original human being. It is like taking a thief to be your son, like taking a brick for a mirror, like taking brass for real gold. This is the fundamental ignorance

underlying birth and death. It is like being a corpse that is still breathing. You cannot release your own radiant light, illumine the self within and shine through the mountains, rivers, and earth.

Even if great awakening is realized and the body of   92
reality is clearly comprehended, if you are polluted by practice and attainment, the Buddha Way does not become manifest. You should know that there is that which is beyond even the beyond.

As for the Zen of the living exemplars, even if a clear   93
mirror is placed on a stand, they break through it right away. Even if a precious pearl is in their palm, they smash it at once. A mortar flies through space, the eastern mountains walk on the water. Having the fortune to know that all living beings have Buddha-nature and that there is already a matter of utmost importance right where you stand, investigate continuously, twenty-four hours a day, in principle and in fact: what is it that is walking, what is it that is sitting, what is it that acts, what is the mind?

If you forge bravely and powerfully ahead, wholeheart-   94
edly questioning and wondering for three to five years without flagging, the Great Wonder will inevitably occur and you will not fail to awaken.

Yet even though you may attain a thoroughgoing great   95
awakening, know that the vast ocean of Buddhism grows deeper the further you enter. If you think there is no enlightenment to attain and no community of living beings to be liberated, if you think the scriptures of the canon are toilet paper and the seventeen hundred koans are worthless, after all you are not really free and at ease; your perception is not liberated, you have not yet passed through the Zen

barrier, and the thieving mind has not died. In this condition, if you do not throw away pride and conceit and quickly realize your error, you will fall into the deep pit of the two vehicles and cut off the life of wisdom of the Buddhas and Zen founders.

96   Nurturing the embryo of sagehood, cultivating practice in the aftermath of awakening, is really not easy. An ancient said, "If your potential does not leave a fixed position, it falls into an ocean of poison." It is imperative to know that there is cultivation on top of realization and to preserve the Way of living Zen with hidden practice and secret application.

97   Do not make the mistake of maintaining the idea of having gained something, lest you become a hungry ghost forever keeping watch over a treasure, or a starveling with a hoard of wealth. Even if you see a Buddha-land manifest and perceive the realm of Buddha, you see only once, not twice.

98   I hope you will concentrate and let go as you breathe out and in, remove all leakage from the stream of mindfulness, perpetuate the bones and marrow of the Buddhas and Zen founders, dispense the pure teaching, like sweet elixir, for the benefit and salvation of all living beings, gratefully requiting the deep and far-reaching blessings you have received.

NOTES

2. *The Ten Stages Scripture* is one of the core texts of the Ekayana ("One Vehicle," or Unitary) school of Buddhism, containing the seeds of all Buddhist teachings. The teaching of the ten stages is referred to as the Alphabet of Buddhism. See *The Flower Ornament Scripture* (Boston: Shambhala Publications, 1984–87), book 26.

4. *The Scripture Spoken by Vimalakīrti* is an important and popular text of the introductory phase of the universalist teachings of Buddhism, of which the aforementioned Unitary school is both the source and culmination. According to the scripture, Vimalakīrti was a householding Buddha who lived in the "time" of Shākyamuni Gautama Buddha.

   True thusness refers to the real character of things, apart from our subjective descriptions and interpretations of what we perceive.

5. *birthlessness* This term refers to the ungraspability of ultimate origins, experiential realization of which spontaneously eliminates mental fixation on appearances. This passage gives a way to actualize the subjective counterpart of objective reality.

6. *The Diamond Cutter Scripture* is one of the most popular Buddhist texts. It is of the *Prajñāpāramitā* or Transcendent Insight corpus of scriptures, which emphasize meaningful action without attachment to appearances.

10. *"Even if . . . virtuous deeds"* This passage refers to the *Ekayana* teaching of *The Lotus of Truth Scripture*, which says that all of those who have done the slightest good deed, even so much

as absentmindedly drawing a picture of Buddha, have all attained Buddhahood. Although it may appear superficial to some, this is a surface of one of the broadest and deepest of Buddhist teachings, that of universal Buddha-nature inherent in all sentient beings.

11. *The Nirvana Scripture* is a vast collection of teachings represented as having been recited and recapitulated while Shākyamuni Gautama Buddha was passing away into *mahāparinirvāna*, the ultimate extinction.

   "The Buddha does not preach anything" means that Buddhist teachings are expedient techniques, not fixed dogma: they are products of enlightenment designed to lead to awakening; they are not themselves enlightenment or awakening. This distinction is critical in the actual practical application of Buddhism.

14. These symbols in *The Lotus of Truth Scripture* represent the universal Buddha-nature inherent in all beings, by virtue of which fundamental enlightenment is accessible to all conscious creatures who become aware of this subtle nature.

16. *"How wonderful"* that *"we ordinary mortals"* have such potential; *"how miserable"* that we ordinarily do not use it.

17. *The Scripture on Visualization of Infinite Life* is one of the three core texts of Chinese Pure Land Buddhism. This scripture contains an elaborate series of visualizations and meditations for mastery of mind, but the key point of the scripture is that "when you see Buddha, you are seeing mind; for mind is Buddha, mind makes Buddha."

20. *eighty-four thousand doctrines* Buddhist teachings are so many and diverse as to be conventionally described as numbering eighty-four thousand, or even more, up to an infinite number. These numbers are also symbolic of the multitude of psychological afflictions, complications, and confusions that Buddhism is designed to cure.

three vehicles These are different levels of Buddhist principles and practices, encompassing both individual liberation and collective salvation.

eightfold path One of the basic formulations of Buddhist practice: right perception, thought, speech, action, livelihood, effort, recollection, and concentration.

27. Ignorant activism may be well-intentioned, but it is inherently limited.

32. Chapter 5 of *The Nirvana Scripture* on the indestructible body says, "The body of the one who has realized thusness is permanently stable and indestructible. It is not a human or divine body, not an insecure body, not a body fed by material food." The text goes on to negate all sorts of conceivable descriptions of attributes of the body of realization.

    Chapter 12 of *The Scripture Spoken by Vimalakīrti*, on seeing the Immovable Buddha (Akshobhya), says, "See the Buddha as you see the real character of your own being. I see the Buddha does not come from the past or go to the future or dwell in the present." This text also goes on to refute all sorts of possible imaginations or conceptions about Buddha, so as to lead to the independent perception of the mind-Buddha, or Buddha-mind.

33. *The Four Reliances* are classical principles for the understanding of Buddhist scriptures, enunciated in *The Nirvana Scripture*:

    1. Rely on principle, not personality.
    2. Rely on the meaning, not the letter.
    3. Rely on objective knowledge, not subjective consciousness.
    4. Rely on a complete teaching, not an incomplete teaching.

34. The great Chan master Linji said that people who formally become monks or nuns but have emotional attachments to their state have merely "left one home to enter another."

Notes

MODELS FOR SITTING MEDITATION

1. It is critical to note that "letting go" of everything is to be done only after establishing the basic orientation of universal compassion and selfless dedication. Many people who fail to attain higher results of meditation are unsuccessful because they inwardly regard this orientation as doctrine and not practice, thus treating the act of vowing as a ritual behavior or a conventional routine. This kind of vow has no power to summon higher awareness.

2. *Then and only then* The author uses an expression that specifies the aforementioned attitude and vow as a necessary precondition for "letting go."

   body and mind are one suchness Body and mind are experienced as a single continuity, which is beyond conceptualization and therefore can only be described as "such" or "as is."

   there is no gap between movement and stillness The ultimate focus of attention remains the same regardless of internal or external movement or stillness.

3. To deliberately deprive oneself of food or sleep, thinking these to be ascetic exercise, may only serve to strengthen attachment to self-importance, besides injuring the physical organism for no good reason. There are Taoist practices of fasting and sleeplessness, but they are dangerous and never done by sensible or directed people without adequate mental and physical preparation.

4. *a quiet, uncluttered place* A place that is both psychologically and physically "quiet," not a circus of imaginations in a hall of ostentation.

5. It is dangerous to force this posture. Western models of athletic training and competition are out of place here. The ancients did not use the lotus posture to cause themselves discomfort. The critical alignments are noted in number 7.

Sitting straight in a chair, standing still, walking, and lying on the right side are also commonly used meditation postures.

6. The arc of the thumbs and fingers form a loop; this particular symbol is called the sign of the cosmos.

7. Rocking back and forth and right and left is for the purpose of helping the body sense a central balance.

A stupa is a Buddhist tomb or reliquary structure. Stupas were originally hemispherical mounds, but in the Far East they were also built as multistoried towers. Here it is the image of a multistoried tower, each story evenly supporting the ones above, to which the author refers. Beginners who still retain a complete sense of physical solidity may even use this image of being a reliquary tower as a visualization to help attain abstraction.

One of the most famous images in Mahāyāna (Great Vehicle, or Universalist) Buddhism is that of a stupa emerging from the ground and opening up to reveal an ancient, extinct Buddha within, miraculously still alive. The emerging of the stupa from the earth is the emerging of potential based on groundwork practices, such as the vowing already mentioned. The opening of the stupa is the electrification of the spiritual spine and brain, the opening of the derelict potential left unused, even trapped, untapped by conventional education and training.

8. *Fayun Yuantong* was one of the most eminent Chan masters of Song dynasty China.

ghost cave in a mountain of darkness A metaphor for oblivion or absorption in nothingness; often used as a term of scorn for repressive concentration and false "emptiness."

9. *Eventually you forget mental objects and spontaneously become unified.* "Eventually" means that it does not help to rush; "you forget mental objects and spontaneously become unified" means that what fragments the mind is the habit of dwelling on objects, which includes thoughts and feelings.

10. *many people do it in a pathological manner* This is why meditation practice and experience cannot really be evaluated in such terms as clock and calendar time; if the inspiration, orientation, or method is off balance, the more meditation is practiced the further it exaggerates such flaws.

11. *using the wind to blow on the fire* Authentically practiced, this kind of meditation amounts to using a natural capacity in order to foster an inherent potential.

12. *when the way is lofty, demons abound* Complacency and conceit make the mind especially vulnerable to obsession; evident attainment makes the individual a target of envy and jealousy. See also next note.

13. *The* Shurangama-sutra *(Heroic March Scripture)* This is a special text closely studied by Chinese Chan Buddhists of the post-classical era, from the Song dynasty onward. In this scripture, Buddha says, "You should know that the subtle illumination in all creatures in the contaminated world, the substance of mind completely aware, is not separate and not apart from that of the Buddhas of the ten directions.

"Because of the mistakes of your false ideas missing the truth, folly and infatuation arise. Because they produce total illusion, there is a false reality. By unceasing transmutation of illusion, the worlds of being are born. Thus all the worlds in the ten directions that are not uncontaminated, numerous as atoms, are defined by deluded, ignorant, false ideas.

"You should know that space itself arises within your mind, like a fleck of cloud dotting a clear sky, to say nothing of the worlds in space! When one individual discovers reality and returns to the source, the entirety of space, in all ten directions, completely vanishes; how could the worlds in space not be shaken apart!

"When you practice meditation and cultivate concentration, the enlightening beings in the ten directions, as well as the great uncontaminated saints, all commune, and there is profound peace right on the spot. All the demon kings, ghosts, spirits, and mundane celestials see their palaces crumble for no apparent reason; their ground quakes and splits, every creature in their water and on their land flies and bounds, all of them startled and frightened.

"Ordinary people, in the dark, do not notice any change. Those others, however, all have five kinds of psychic power, lacking only the power of freedom from all contamination. Being fondly attached to these experiences and passions of theirs, how could they let you smash their abodes? For this reason, spirits, ghosts, celestial demons, devils, and sprites will all come to disturb you in your concentration.

"However, even though the demons may have tremendous wrath in their passions, in your subtle awareness it is like wind blowing on light, like a sword slicing through water; they do not touch each other. You are like boiling water, they are like solid ice; as warmth gradually gets nearer, before long ice melts."

Tiantai manuals of "stopping and seeing" There are four Tiantai Buddhist meditation classics under this rubric, known as the *Small*, the *Great*, the *Gradual*, and *Unfixed Stopping and Seeing*. As used in a general way in Far Eastern Buddhism, based on the classics of Tiantai Buddhism, *stopping* means stopping confusion; *seeing* means observing realities. In the Tiantai manuals of stopping and seeing, there appear very concrete descriptions of demonic hallucinations.

Guifeng's Guidelines Guifeng Zongmi, who died in the mid-ninth century, was a prolific writer on the original teachings and original practices of Chan Buddhism. He is also considered a patriarch of the Chinese Flower Ornament school of Buddhism. Most of his work is lost.

Those whose preparation is insufficient One of the functions of literature on meditation is to prepare the mind for the experiences—authentic and delusive—that await consciousness beyond the boundaries of ordinary awareness.

17. *to die sitting or pass away standing* Many ancient meditation masters are reported to have died sitting or to have passed away standing, without illness, as a deliberate act to represent the transcendence of both the allure of life and the crushing power of death. In Sanskrit, nirvana is also called *amrta*, which means "the state where there is no death."

18. *What will you use to counteract karma? Karma* means "action"; in usages like this, it specifically refers to the actions of past and present that create the conditions of bondage in the present and future.

19. The final passage is reconnected to the first passage, forming a circle. The closing of this circle is symbolic of the completion of the cycle of instruction and the beginning of the cycle of application.

GUIDELINES FOR SITTING MEDITATION

1. *If something comes to mind, do your best to cast it away.* There are many different techniques for overcoming the influence of conditioned thoughts, but they may be classified generally into two broad categories corresponding to the Taoist terms *doing* and *nondoing.* The preceding essay presented a method characterized more by "nondoing" than by "doing," whereas this essay has more "doing" to it; even though the deliberate "doing" of overcoming the mesmerism of conditioned thought is practiced for the purpose of attaining spontaneous "nondoing" of compulsive thinking, whereby delusion does not arise even though no deliberate attempt is made to suppress it.

2. This paragraph outlines the practice of cultivating awareness

of the essence of consciousness underlying the functions of consciousness.

3. It is quite possible to be dependent on conceptions without being consciously aware of it, even while in what subjectively seems to be a state of concentration without thought. This is why radical direct introspection and analytic introspection are both employed in Buddhist meditation, supplying a standpoint outside the ordinary subjectivity of the individual as an outlook or observatory from which to view reality at large.

4. *the uncreate* This word expresses the beginningless continuity of infinity, as well as the state of mind under acquiescence to infinity, not creating self-deluding attachments to illusory thoughts.

5. *Joy* at the intimation of Buddhahood within is the first stage of enlightenment according to the comprehensive scheme of the ten stages. See *The Flower Ornament Scripture*, book 26, first part.

6. *The source of realization of enlightenment is the identity of mind, Buddha, and living beings.* This expression of the triplex identity of mind, Buddha, and all beings is a key phrase of *The Flower Ornament Scripture* in the teachings of Chan Buddhism.

7. To *turn things around* means to use things consciously for purposes of enlightenment rather than be deluded and manipulated by them. *The Flower Ornament Scripture* says, "Beings teach, lands teach, all things in all times teach, constantly, without interruption."

   Vimalakīrti is the main teacher in *The Scripture Spoken by Vimalakīrti*, a very important text that teaches the integration of nirvana and samsara in the realm of inconceivable enlightenment.

8. *Otherwise, you will be going around in circles forever.* The meditation taught here is for breaking the chain of routine perception, thought, and behavior.

Notes

A GENERALLY RECOMMENDED MODE OF SITTING
MEDITATION

1. *Cultivation and realization* are ways to bring the human being into harmony with the Way, or objective reality; they are ways to the Way.
2. Again, the need for effort is not because the source of enlightening is not available but because our own subjective conditions make it impossible for us to avail ourselves of the enlightenment of the source.
3. The "wiping clean" process of purification of the mind itself, not attempted removal of objects.
4. *The Scripture of Complete Enlightenment* says, "Complete awareness is my sanctuary." The question of "why" is multifaceted; not only does it suggest practice of meditation wherever we are, it also suggests careful examination of the inner and outer reasons or rationales for emphasizing a particular venue.
5. Here the main answer to all the above questions is given; the answer is in the questions itself, in the subjective condition of the individual; for it is the subjective condition that filters and construes the truths set forth by the author as the setting of each conundrum in this series of questions. For this reason, the questions should not be taken as merely rhetorical.
6. This paragraph warns about what is supposed to happen in the initial stage of realization in the exercise being taught in this treatise. This procedure follows an established pattern of preparing meditators before they plunge into intensive work.

What this passage is referring to is what Japanese Zennists call *kenshō*, "seeing essence," direct conscious experience of the essential nature of mind itself. This brings a feeling of freedom that, compared with the stickiness of mind fascinated by its own functions and productions, is utterly amazing and seems absolute to the inexperienced beginner. A good deal of Dōgen's work is devoted to helping seekers overcome this major obstacle in Zen study, the affliction caused by "light shining right in your eyes," causing a dazzling effect.

Getting beyond this stage, having *a living road of emancipation*, means bringing abstract enlightenment to life in daily activities.

7. *Transmission of the mind seal at Shaolin* refers to Bodhidharma, reputed founder of Chan (Zen) Buddhism in China, who is said to have "faced a wall for nine years." This is an expression referring to cultivation of imperturbability of mind. This immovable mind is described as being like a wall or a sheer cliff.

8. *pursuing words and chasing sayings* In Dōgen's time, academic study of Buddhism was prevalent among Japanese priests, who often pursued it without corresponding meditation or life practice.

stepping back This means disengagement from involvement in thought and its objects.

turning the light around and looking back This means inwardly looking into the source of consciousness rather than outwardly pursuing the products of consciousness.

Body and mind will naturally be shed Ordinary self-awareness is molted.

the original countenance This refers to the pristine essence of mind, and what it directly witnesses.

9. *Do not aim to become a Buddha* Subjective wishes, fantasies, imaginations, conceptions, and ambitions, no matter how seemingly sublime, can all interfere with the process.

how could it be limited to sitting or reclining? The essential technique is mental and does not involve attachment to the body in any way.

10. Again it should be pointed out that forcing the lotus or half-lotus posture does more harm than good, increasing physical egohood rather than decreasing it, expending energy rather than husbanding it.

14–15. This is the exercise of "turning the light around and looking back" mentioned in number 8. For a fuller discussion, see Cleary, *Shōbōgenzō: Zen Essays by Dōgen* (Honolulu: University of Hawaii Press, 1986), pp. 9–13.

16. *not practice of dhyāna* This means that the meditation exercise taught here is not a system of rigidly defined stages and states; it is a direct approach to the essential nature of mind and consciousness and the immediate perception of reality.

18. When rising from intense concentration, it is important to release the mind as well as the body from the intensity of its focus before getting up.

20. The allusions are to old Zen stories of people Buddhistically awakened on seeing or hearing an object, gesture, or utterance in states of pinpoint concentration.

21. This meditation is for awakening a kind of knowledge that is not filtered and formulated by conventional intelligence. The distribution of this knowledge, therefore, does not conform to patterns ordinarily established for other kinds of abstract knowledge.

22. *the process . . . is being normal.* In Zen terms, "normalcy" means the mind as it is in its pristine innocence, without the exaggeration of acquired mental habits.

23. *West and East* The experience of Buddhist enlightenment is not obstructed by cultural differences, because it only takes place after the habit of clinging to views is relinquished.

24. *Just work on sitting* This can be understood both literally and figuratively. People may try all sorts of things as "spiritual exercises," when really they are secretly trying to distract, amuse, or otherwise occupy themselves. This was as rampant in Dōgen's time, relatively speaking, as it is today. The general recommendation here is not to chase after this fad and that but rather to quiet down and look right into the source of everything you are.

25. When you see into the source, you can see what is at hand without illusion or prejudice.
27. Contemplation of impermanence is commonly considered a good way to arouse the aspiration and will for enlightenment.
28. *feel an elephant by hand* This alludes to the ancient story of the blind men and the elephant, referring to the fragmentary nature of studies lacking direct perception of the whole.
29. *Having long been thus, we should be thus.* Buddha-nature is the original mind; having always had the potential for awakening, why not use it?

SECRETS OF CULTIVATING THE MIND

1. *The triple world* This means the conditioned world, comprising three realms: the realm of desire, the realm of form, and the realm of formless abstraction. Buddhist enlightenment involves transcending even the formless realm in order to attain complete freedom.
3. This paragraph refers to a contemplative exercise, not to a metaphysical doctrine or belief.
4. *Dharma* means principle, truth, teaching, or reality.
5. Ascetic practices without essential insight tend to increase egoism and self-absorption rather than diminish it.
6. *The World Honored One* is an epithet of Buddha.
12. *Linji* was a great Chan Buddhist master of ninth-century China. One of the greatest Chan classics consists of a collection of this master's sayings.
14. Faith in the immanent Buddha-nature is not an inculcated belief. It may be deduced, as in this story, but is only realized as a direct experience.
15. Master Guizong was one of the greatest of the early classical Chan masters in Tang dynasty China. He lived in the latter eighth and early ninth centuries.

17. Many people miss opportunities to learn by expecting on-demand displays of what they personally consider to be spiritual and miraculous powers.

18. Rather than making grandiose promises, the author places the emphasis on the need for understanding and preparation.

21. *Guifeng* See note 13 of *Models For Sitting Meditation*.

22. Buddhist sages do not employ extraordinary powers for personal ends; only in pursuit of universal vows.

23. The need for understanding and preparation is exceptionally keen when dealing with attractive ideas like supranormal powers.

24. Many people who think they want enlightenment secretly want thrills. When they are no longer thrilled, they lose interest, not even realizing any enlightenment from this very sequence of events.

27–28. See note number 6 of *A Generally Recommended Mode of Sitting Meditation*.

30. See Cleary, *Shōbōgenzō: Zen Essays by Dōgen*, p. 10.

33. *you are able to use ten thousand ounces of gold in a day*. This means you can live in the world and deal intimately with the things of the world without being afflicted.

38. *Spiritual powers and subtle functions—drawing water and hauling wood.* All actions are productions from an ultimately inconceivable source. The "water and wood," or material being (self and world), as ordinarily conceived are not the spiritual and subtle. The spiritual and subtle are the livingness that "draws" and "hauls."

39–43. The Sound Seer is a supernal bodhisattva (enlightening being) manifesting pure compassion, envisioned as watching the cries of the world. The Sound Seer's gateway into principle, or noumenon, is to focus the attention on the ineffable essence in the faculty of hearing.

47. This series of negatives is also a meditation exercise, to

be worked through mindfully and contemplatively, step by step.

49. *six courses* This term is a traditional general representation of habit-ridden ways of life. The six courses are hungry ghosts, representing greed and craving; titans or antigods, representing conceit, jealousy, resentment, and hatred; animals, representing ignorance and folly; hells, representing a combination of all the above; humanity, representing social conscience and morality; celestial realms, representing higher morality and elevated psychic states. Buddhahood is beyond even the most sublime of the celestial realms.

52. *real faith* Here it is made plain that faith is not fundamentally a conceptual item or habit of thought but a manifestation of connection, however remotely sensed, with the very essence of awareness and being.

55. *five courses of existence* This term means the same thing as the six courses (note 49 above), minus the celestial course. Thus "five courses" is a general way of describing typical routines of habit, compulsion, and bondage.

57. *Master Gao* was the great Chinese Chan master Dahui Zonggao, one of the major workers behind the Song dynasty revival of Chan. See my translations *Zen Lessons: The Art of Leadership* (Boston: Shambhala Publications, 1989) and *Zen Essence: The Science of Freedom* (Boston: Shambhala Publications, 1989) for extensive reports and statements of this master.

58. *ox-herding practice* The mind is likened to an ox; the task of taming the unruly mind is likened to ox herding.

61. *followers* This term refers to followers of Buddhism, specifically those who try to annihilate passion to attain nirvana.

62. This is the morality of nondoing; do not dwell on the impulse or elaborate the thought and the act will not be forthcoming. See "Do Not Do Any Evil" in my *Rational Zen: The Mind of Dōgen Zenji* (Boston: Shambhala Publications, 1993).

63. *six sense fields* The power of mind to organize elementary sense data is also considered a sense, the sixth sense.

68. *Caoqi* (Ts'ao-ch'i) This refers to the illustrious Sixth Patriarch of Chan Buddhism, who died in the early eighth century.

91. *eight winds* Eight influences that ordinarily affect people: gain and loss, praise and blame, honor and censure, pleasure and pain.

   three kinds of sensation Pleasant, painful, neutral.

93. *stones placed on grass* This is a metaphor for practicing repression of thought; it temporarily inhibits growth but is not permanent.

98. *The Secret of Mind Alone* This is a short work by the great Buddhist author Yanshou (ninth to tenth century). Master of the four major schools of Chinese Buddhism, patriarch of both Chan and Pure Land schools, Yanshou's work was very influential in Korea.

99. *good friends* Buddha said, "When you travel, go with those who are better than you, or at least equal. If there are none, go alone; do not travel in the company of fools." Finding good friends is a matter of how you look for them.

100. *blind tortoise/minute seed* These expressions are traditional metaphors: the rarity of meeting a true teaching is as that of the chances of a blind tortoise in the middle of the ocean coming upon a piece of driftwood; the difficulty of meeting your true teacher is said to be as that of a tiny seed dropped from the highest sky landing on the tip of a needle on the face of the earth. The implication here is that if you pay no attention to this treatise, when do you imagine you will find such an opportunity?

104. *the four realizations* These are the consummations of four stages of individual liberation: having entered the stream (of Buddhist awareness), returning once (to the mundane world before release), never returning, and entering nirvana.

Notes

107. *"I cannot do anything for those who do not ask themselves what to do."* This is a famous quotation from Confucius.

112. *skin bag* This term refers to the physical body.

ABSORPTION IN THE TREASURY OF LIGHT

1. *Shōbōgenzō* is a large collection of essays by Dōgen Zenji, the Zen teacher of the author of the present treatise.

2. *unobstructive application of inconspicuous practice* This is a technical expression referring to practice that is purely mental in essence and has no outwardly perceptible form. Its influence on others is also ethereal, not nonexistent in spite of being unexpressed on ordinary cognitive terms.

3. *three bodies* This is a technical term for three facets of Buddhahood: the reality body, corresponding to essence; the enjoyment body, corresponding to knowledge; and the emanation body, corresponding to action.

   four knowledges This term refers to four facets of the consciousness of Buddhas: the mirrorlike knowledge, seeing things as "such," impartially, like a mirror reflecting whatever is before it; the knowledge of equality, which sees things in terms of their universal essential nature; the analytic observing knowledge, which sees things in terms of their individual functions, characteristics, and appearances; and practical knowledge, which sees things in terms of composition and effect.

   states of absorption numerous as atoms in every aspect of reality This expression refers to any and all possible knowledge, consciousness, perception, and awareness.

   The Flower Ornament Scripture All of the chapters of this scripture in which Buddha has gone to visit a heavenly realm are especially important in Zen study.

4. *Lamplike Illuminate* The Buddha Dīpankāra, an ancient Buddha

whose name means "lamp," often translated into Chinese as Burning Lamp for effect. Dīpaṇkāra is very important in Buddhist symbolic mythology as the buddha in whose presence Shākyamuni, or Gautama Buddha, the historical Buddha, was originally inspired to seek unexcelled complete perfect enlightenment.

5. *"Thus once I heard"* This refers to the traditional opening of Buddhist scriptures, and represents perceiving things just as they are, without subjective distortion of reception.

8–11. *Vairochana* "The Illuminator," or "the Great Sun Buddha," is the name of the primordial reality-body Buddha in esoteric Buddhism; in Flower Ornament Buddhism, Vairochana is the transcendent personality of the historical Buddha and also a representation of the eternal enlightenment of Buddhahood.

13. *Awakening by Light* See *The Flower Ornament Scripture*, book 9. Mañjushri represents wisdom and knowledge.

16. *Maitreya* The Buddha of the Future.

20–22. See *The Blue Cliff Record* (Boston: Shambhala Publications, 1977), chapter 1.

24–28. See *The Blue Cliff Record*, chapter 86.

26. See *No Barrier: Unlocking the Zen Koan* (New York: Bantam, 1993), chapter 45.

30. See *No Barrier*, chapter 39.

38. *ghost cave* This technical term ordinarily refers to blanking the mind.

    count the grains of sand This expression refers to intellectualistic literalism without the spirit of the teaching.

    mosquitoes breaking through a paper window Reciting ("buzzing") without understanding.

39. *wash a clod of earth in the mud* This expression means to try to resolve delusive thoughts by conceptual elaboration.

40. *Changsha* was one of the greatest masters of the classical era of Chan.

43. *child of a rich family but has no britches.* All people have the fundamental intelligence known as Buddha-nature but are ordinarily unable to avail themselves of it.

45. Some of these delusions can be extremely subtle, so they are pointed out forcefully to call attention to them.

48. *holeless iron hammerhead* A traditional metaphor, in this case meaning that there is no way to grasp it, yet it is effective.

49. See *No Barrier*, chapter 19.

59. *Puning Yong* was a Song dynasty Chan master of the Linji school.

65. *Yongjia* was a Tiantai Buddhist meditation master also recognized as a spiritual heir of the Sixth Patriarch of Chan. In the Zen schools he is called the Overnight Enlightened Guest because he was so aware that he needed only one day with the Patriarch to complete his awakening.

   Nāgārjuna An Indian Buddhist master who lived from around 100 BCE to about 100 CE. He is considered the fourteenth Indian ancestor of Chan Buddhism and is especially famous for his work on emptiness and transcendent wisdom. See Keizan's *Transmission of Light* (San Francisco: North Point Press, 1990), chapter 15.

66–67. *lowly hireling/pauper/cesspool cleaner* These are all images from *The Lotus Scripture* (another major scripture ordinarily studied by Chan and Zen Buddhists) representing those alienated from inherent Buddha-nature, thus enslaved to externals.

73. *Shaolin* is the name of a temple; here it refers to Bodhidharma, the founder of Chan in China, who lived at Shaolin temple for a time.

76. *four debts* These are the debts one owes to one's parents, to all living beings, to society, and to the Three Treasures (the Buddha, the Teaching, and the Harmonious Community).

77. *Caoshan (Ts'ao-shan)* A ninth-century Chan master, one of the great teachers of the classical era of Chan. See *Timeless Spring:*

A Sōtō Zen Anthology, translated by Thomas Cleary (New York: Weatherhill 1980).

95. *Baizhang (Pai-chang)* A great master of the classical era of Chan, said to have drafted the original rules for Chan communes, Baizhang died in the early ninth century. See *Sayings and Doings of Pai-Chang, Ch'an Master of Great Wisdom*, translated by Thomas Cleary (Los Angeles: Center Publications, 1978).

98. *samsara* Commonly translated into Chinese as "birth and death," "turning in circles," this term means routine existence.

101. *seven Buddhas* This refers to a lineage of seven ancient Buddhas, the seventh being Shākyamuni (Gautama) Buddha, the historical Buddha. This lineage represents the ancient and timeless roots of the teaching, the buddhist Dharma.

107. *the sitting of the two vehicles* The two vehicles (known as "hearers" and "those awake to conditioning") are courses of individual liberation. Their "sitting" refers to one-sided inclination to nirvana as quiescence. See number 119.

108. *the empty fist* Buddhist teachings are likened to an empty fist holding an imaginary gift to pacify a crying child; that is, the teachings are only expedient means of bringing about a calculated effect, not absolute dogma to be worshipped as sacred in themselves.

110–112. This is why Chan masters in China traditionally warned people to cultivate their own perception before trying to look for a "teacher" to guide them spiritually.

118. The careerist model does not apply to enlightenment.

AN ELEMENTARY TALK ON ZEN

1. Compare this passage with numbers 1 through 4 of *A Generally Recommended Mode of Sitting Meditation*.

8. *Don't think/don't seek* Meditation practice involves total absorption in the recitation itself, without anticipating results.

10. *kill* In Zen parlance, this means to transcend, or detach from something.

    seven consciousnesses This term refers to the consciousnesses of the six senses, plus a faculty for judgement and evaluation.

21. *iron walls* This refers to constrictions of consciousness.

    Polar Mountain This stands for the gravitational center of the surface plane of a mundane world. To walk over the Polar Mountain means "to overcome the world," to become free from the magnetic pull of worldliness.

22. *and* 26. Many people profess to believe that familial and social responsibilities conflict with meditation.

23. Again the powerful exercise of contemplating impermanence is recommended for developing the will for enlightenment.

32. *two truths* The two truths, absolute and relative, are that phenomena are empty of absolute identity yet exist in a temporary and conditional way.

    The Middle Way This refers to central balance between extremes, such as of emptiness and existence, rejection and attachment.

40. *ocean of energy/field of elixir* These terms refer to two sensitive points in the body below the navel, commonly used as points of focus in Taoist energetics. It is not good to focus too intently on a precise point, except for special curative purposes; filling the entire lower body with energy is the general idea here. For special instructions concerning female practitioners, see my *Immortal Sisters: Secrets of Taoist Women* (Boston: Shambhala Publications, 1989).

44. *"the bottom falls out of the bucket"* This expression means that the sense of "me" as a solid entity vanishes, the limiting encasement of the ego dissolves, and the mind is freed.

    "kick over the alchemical furnace" At this stage "the furnace"

stands for the body; to kick it over means to transcend the feeling of physical selfhood clinging to the body.

passing beyond myriad aeons in a single instant This expression refers to consciousness disentangled from the temporally conditioned worldview, which includes views of time and space. When consciousness is no longer bound to the parameters of views, it is free.

Prajñātāra This figure is represented as the twenty-seventh Indian ancestor of Zen. See *The Book of Serenity*, chapter 3.

46. See my translation of Dōgen's *Record of Things Heard* (Boulder, Colo.: Prajna Press, 1980), p. 71.

47. See *Immortal Sisters* and my translation of Chang Po-tuan's *The Inner Teachings of Taoism* (Boston: Shambhala Publications, 1986).

48. See the chapter on Chang San-feng in my *Vitality Energy Spirit: A Taoist Sourcebook* (Boston: Shambhala Publications, 1991).

53. *six bandits* This term refers to the objects of the six senses, spoken of in reference to their capacity to "steal" attention and "rob" people of energy.

four demons This term refers to four types of "demons" or "devils" that can "kill the life of wisdom." The four demons are the demon of the body-mind clusters (form, feeling, perception, conditioning, consciousness); the demon of afflictions (such as greed, hatred, folly, vanity, opinionated views); the demon of death; and the "heavenly devil," or the capacity for endless self-deception.

57. *three poisons* Greed, hatred, and folly.

five desires Desires for the objects of the five basic senses.

59–66. Zen teachers of all times left many indications by which interested seekers might discern authenticity or otherwise in reputed or supposed manifestations of Zen practice or teaching.

70. *elixir of five energies* This is a Taoist term for the concentration,

congealment, and crystallization of energy. The number *five* refers to five basic elements or forces; to concentrate and crystallize them together means to recollect and pool the total energy available to the body and mind.

81. *Yunmen* One of the most distinguished classical Chinese Chan masters.

    Ninagawa Shinzaemon A friend and disciple of the famous Japanese Zen master Ikkyu.

    The Shogun Takauji Fourteenth-century founder of the second military government in Japan, a noted student and patron of Zen.

93. *A mortar flies through space, the eastern mountains walk on the water.* These expressions refer to the realm of experience in which everything is inconceivable yet evident.

95. *the deep pit of the two vehicles* This expression refers to attachment to detachment.